Lab Manual for

CCNA Guide to Cisco Networking,

Second Edition

Kelly Cannon

THOMSON

COURSE TECHNOLOGY

Australia • Canada • Mexico • Singapore • Spain • United Kingdom • United States

THOMSON
™
COURSE TECHNOLOGY

Lab Manual for CCNA Guide to Cisco Networking, Second Edition
is published by Course Technology

Associate Publisher:
Steve Elliot

Acquisitions Editor:
William Pitkin, III

Product Manager:
Amy M. Lyon

Developmental Editor:
Jill Batistick

Production Editor:
Anne Valsangiacomo

Technical Editor:
Robert Butler

Quality Assurance Tester:
Jeremy Cioara

Senior Manufacturing Coordinator:
Laura Burns

Product Marketing Manager:
Jason Sakos

Associate Product Manager:
Tim Gleeson

Editorial Assistant:
Nick Lombardi

Cover Design:
Julie Malone

Text Designer:
GEX Publishing Services

Compositor:
GEX Publishing Services

BRIEF CONTENTS

Table of Contents

INTRODUCTION

Hands-on learning is the best way to master the networking skills necessary for both the CCNA exam and a career in wide-area networking. This book contains more than 50 hands-on exercises that apply networking concepts, such as IP addressing, routing, and switching, as they would be applied on Cisco equipment in the real world and on CCNA exam 640-607. In addition, each chapter offers multiple review questions to reinforce mastery of the CCNA topics.

The organization of this lab manual follows the same organization as Course Technology's *CCNA Guide to Cisco Networking, Second Edition*, and using the two together will provide a substantial, effective learning experience.

This book is suitable for use in any Cisco CCNA course. As a prerequisite, students should have basic networking knowledge, such as the skills learned in an introductory networking course.

FEATURES

In order to ensure a successful experience for instructors and students alike, this book includes the following sections for each lab:

- **Lab Objectives:** Every lab has a brief description and list of learning objectives.

- **Materials Required:** Every lab includes information on hardware, software, and other materials you will need to complete the lab.

- **Estimated Completion Time:** Every lab has an estimated completion time, so that you can plan your activities accurately.

- **Activity:** The actual lab activity is presented in this section. Logical and precise step-by-step instructions guide you through the lab.

- **Certification Objectives:** Each chapter lists the relevant objectives from Cisco's CCNA exam 640-607.

- **Review Questions:** Every lab provides follow-up questions to help reinforce concepts presented in the lab.

HARDWARE REQUIREMENTS

The following is a list of hardware required to complete all the labs in the book. The hardware requirements for many of the individual labs are less than what is listed. In terms of routers and switches, if you have a Cisco Academy CCNA lab setup, you have the necessary equipment for the labs in Chapter 6 through the end of the book.

The hardware required for Chapters 1 through 5 is minimal. The routing and switching lab setup, in addition to any other hardware required, is as follows:

- Six computers running Microsoft Windows 98, Windows XP, Windows NT, or Windows 2000, with NICs installed
- HyperTerminal installed on all Windows computers
- One Windows Internet computer with a NIC configured and the TCP/IP protocol configured
- One CSU/DSU (you can substitute a router if necessary and it doesn't have to work; it is for simulation purposes only)
- One bridge (doesn't have to work; it is for simulation purposes only)
- Transceivers for the router Ethernet ports if these Ethernet ports use an AUI connection instead of RJ-45
- Transceivers for the bridge connections if the bridge uses AUI connections instead of RJ-45
- Three hubs
- Nine NIC cards with RJ-45 transceivers to simulate nine host computers
- Nineteen UTP patch cables
- One serial cable with a compatible connector for a serial interface on a router on one end and a v.35 connector on the other end to attach to the CSU/DSU. If another router will be used instead of the CSU/DSU, the cable connector should match the serial interface on the additional router.
- A box or spool of Cat 5 UTP cable
- One UTP cable crimper and one pair of wire cutters for every four students
- Box of RJ-45 connectors
- One UTP continuity tester (or other cable tester) for every four students
- Thinnet sample
- Thicknet sample
- Category 5 UTP sample

- Category 3 UTP sample
- Multimode fiber sample
- Single-mode fiber sample
- STP sample
- 1 T-connector
- RJ-45 connector
- 1 RG-58 terminator
- Plenum cable sample
- One patch panel for every four students, preferably mounted on a rack to hold it steady
- One Krone tool or other punchdown tool for every four students
- Several properly made UTP patch cables for testing
- Four, 2501 series routers with power cables (could substitute a different series but must have two serial interfaces and one Ethernet interface)
- One, 2514 series router with power cable (could substitute a different series but must have two serial interfaces and two Ethernet interface)
- One or two Cisco series 1900 switch (or other appropriate series switch) with power cord
- Five hubs with power cables (can substitute switches)
- Three V.35 DTE cables (male) with serial end to match serial interface on routers
- Three V.35 DCE cables (female) with serial end to match serial interface on routers
- Six Ethernet 10BaseT UTP to AUI transceivers (will not need these if the Ethernet interfaces on the routers are RJ-45 transceivers)
- Five RJ-45 to RJ-45 rollover cables
- Five RJ-45 to DB-25 or DB-9 connectors
- Power strips
- UTP patch cable
- TFTP server software on a diskette (preferably Cisco's, which is TFTPSERV.EXE)
- A rollover cable for the switch
- A folder named SWITCHTEST containing enough files to equal at least 100 MB on the desktops of the lab-b, lab-d, and lab-e computers
- A stopwatch

ACKNOWLEDGEMENTS

I would like to thank Course Technology for the opportunity to be involved in the world of academic publishing. I would especially like to thank Jill Batistick, the Development Editor, for her attention to detail and Robert Butler, the Technical Editor, for agreeing to catch my mistakes. In addition, I am grateful to Amy Lyon for all of her hard work on this project. Thanks also to Jeremy Cioara for helping with the Quality Assurance testing, and to all of the reviewers who worked under exceptionally tight deadlines and gave consistently great feedback: Rob Andrews, Pittsburgh Technical Institute; Anthony Cameron, Fayetteville Technical Community College; Jeremy Graves, Jones County Junior College; and Tim Powers, University of Alaska, Juneau.

Foremost and finally, I would like to thank my always supportive family: Jim, Veronica, and Adrienne.

INTRODUCING NETWORKS

Labs included in this chapter

➤ Lab 1.1 Understanding the OSI Model
➤ Lab 1.2 Understanding the Five Steps of Data Encapsulation
➤ Lab 1.3 Identifying Data Link and Network Layer Addresses
➤ Lab 1.4 Connection-Oriented Versus Connectionless Communications

CCNA Exam Objectives

Objective	Lab
Identify at least three reasons why the industry uses a layered model	1.1
List the key internetworking functions for the OSI Network layer	1.1, 1.2
Define and explain the five conversion steps of data encapsulation	1.2
Describe Data Link and Network addresses and identify key differences between them	1.3
Define and describe the function of the MAC address	1.3
Describe connection-oriented network service and connectionless network service, and identify their key differences	1.4

LAB 1.1 UNDERSTANDING THE OSI MODEL

Objectives

Within the networking world, the OSI seven-layer model has been widely adopted. This adoption has facilitated the teaching of networking principles and the development of networking software and hardware. The OSI seven-layer model is an open standard that has been accepted worldwide. The goal of this lab is to make sure you understand what happens at each of the seven layers so that you are successful as a network troubleshooter and as a CCNA candidate.

After completing this lab, you will be able to:

➤ Identify the OSI model layer associated with various network functions

➤ Describe the reasons for using the layered model

Materials Required

This lab requires the following:

➤ A pen or pencil

Estimated completion time: **30 minutes**

ACTIVITY

1. Relate the following networking descriptions to their correct OSI layer number by placing them in the correct cell in the Description column of Table 1-1. There may be more than one term or phrase for each layer.

- Bits
- Where communications begin
- End-to-end transmission
- CSMA/CD
- Compression
- Logical address
- Signals
- Request for network services
- Duplex
- CRC
- LLC

- Frames
- Encoding
- NIC software functions
- Synchronization
- Voltage
- Services to applications
- Internetwork travel
- SQL
- Data segmentation
- Connectionless service

- Datagram
- Cable
- Best path selection
- MAC address
- Formatting
- ACK
- Hubs
- ASCII
- Encryption
- MTU

Table 1-1   OSI model layer functions

OSI Layer	Description
Application	
Presentation	
Session	
Transport	
Network	
Data Link	
Physical	

Certification Objectives

Objectives for the CCNA exam:

➤ Identify at least three reasons why the industry uses a layered model

➤ List the key internetworking functions for the OSI Network layer

Review Questions

1. How does using the OSI model facilitate teaching and learning about networking?

2. How does using the OSI model facilitate the development of networking hardware and software?

3. How does using the OSI model provide compatibility and standardization between networking products?

4. How does the user fit into the OSI model?

5. What is the importance of the Network layer?

6. At which layer do the ultimate sender and receiver of data make contact?

7. If, when you are browsing the web, the networking cable gets pulled out of the computer, the connection to the web site can often be restored if you plug the cable back in. Which layer is responsible for maintaining the connection?

8. What are the two sublayers of the Data Link layer? Which one is closest to the Physical layer?

9. What is meant by "peer communication" with respect to the OSI model?

10. Is networking software more closely related to the upper layers or lower layers of the OSI model?

LAB 1.2 UNDERSTANDING THE FIVE STEPS OF DATA ENCAPSULATION

Objectives

During transport from the source node to the destination node, data makes its way down the protocol stack and is wrapped, or enclosed, at each layer by a header. This wrapping is called encapsulation.

There are five steps of data encapsulation during the data's journey from the application layer through the physical layer. The goal of this lab is to make sure you understand what happens at each of the five steps. Remember that this process begins with the user initiating network resources. This is at the top of the OSI model.

After completing this lab, you will be able to:

➤ Define encapsulation in terms of networking

➤ Describe the five steps of data encapsulation

Materials Required

This lab requires the following:

➤ A pen or pencil

Estimated completion time: **15 minutes**

ACTIVITY

1. The following bulleted list contains data encapsulation descriptions. Match these descriptions to their correct step numbers by placing them in the correct cell in the Description column of Table 1-2. There may be more than one term or phrase for each step.

   ■ Conversion to standard data format
   ■ Encoding
   ■ Frame
   ■ Datagram
   ■ Maximum transmission units
   ■ Logical address
   ■ Bit transmission
   ■ Upper layers
   ■ IP header
   ■ Trailer
   ■ Segments
   ■ Packet creation
   ■ Pulses
   ■ Physical address

2. For each step number in Table 1-2, give the associated OSI model layer(s).

Table 1-2   Data encapsulation

Step Number	Description	Associated OSI Model Layer(s)
1		
2		
3		
4		
5		

Certification Objectives

Objectives for the CCNA exam:

➤ Define and explain the five conversion steps of data encapsulation

➤ List the key internetworking functions for the OSI Network layer

Review Questions

1. Which layers of the OSI model are involved in data encapsulation?

2. Which layers generally constitute the upper layers of the OSI model?

3. Encapsulation is often called "wrapping." Why?

4. During the encapsulation process, do upper layers provide services for the layers below them or do lower layers provide services for layers above them?

5. What is the most common logical address used in networking today?

6. What is another name for the physical address?

7. What is a maximum transmission unit?

8. What is the process of encoding?

9. What is a PDU?

10. How does the Network layer facilitate data encapsulation?

LAB 1.3 IDENTIFYING DATA LINK AND NETWORK LAYER ADDRESSES

Objectives

Networks use two different kinds of addresses: physical addresses at the Data Link layer and logical addresses at the Network layer. Typically, the physical address is a MAC address and the logical address is an IP address. The goal of this lab is finding and identifying these different addresses on a Windows computer and defining the purpose of a MAC address. The MAC address is also known as the physical address because it is burned onto the NIC card during the manufacturing process. A NIC card and a MAC address are shown in Figure 1-1.

Network
interface card
(NIC)

MAC address
00-00-00-21-43-77

⌣   ⌣

OUI   Serial #

Figure 1-1   MAC address and NIC card

After completing this lab, you will be able to:

➤ Describe Data Link and Network addresses and identify key differences between them

➤ Define and describe the function of the MAC address

Materials Required

This lab requires the following:

➤ A computer running Microsoft Windows 98, Windows NT, Windows 2000, or Windows XP, with Internet access

Estimated completion time: **20 minutes**

ACTIVITY

1. Turn on the computer.

2. Click **Start**, point to **Programs**, and then click **MS-DOS Prompt** (**Command Prompt** replaces MS-DOS prompt on NT and 2000 computers).

3. Type the command **ipconfig /all** at the DOS prompt, press **Enter**, and then answer the following questions:

a. What type of NIC card is in the computer?

1

b. What is the MAC (adapter) address?

00-50-BA-C8-1F-C4

c. Which part of the MAC address is the OUI?

The first 3 row of numbers

d. Which part of the MAC address is the serial number?

the last 3 row of numbers

e. What is the IP address?

172.16.0.40

f. What is the subnet mask?

255.255.0.0

g. What is the default gateway?

172.16.0.1

4. Close the DOS window.

5. Open a web browser, type **http://standards.ieee.org/regauth/oui** in the Address box, and then press **Enter**.

6. In the OUI Search For: text box, type **Cisco**, and then press **Enter**.

7. What is one of the six digit OUI codes for Cisco?

00-00-0C

8. Repeat Step 6 and search for **3COM**.

9. What is one of the six digit OUI codes for 3COM?

00-01-01

10. Close the browser window.

Certification Objectives

Objectives for the CCNA exam:

➤ Describe Data Link and Network addresses and identify key differences between them

➤ Define and describe the function of the MAC address

Review Questions

1. Which layer of the OSI model is associated with the physical address?

2. Who assigns the first six digits of the MAC address?

3. Who assigns the second six digits of the MAC address?

4. What alphanumeric characters are acceptable in a MAC address?

5. What does an IP address look like?

6. Who assigns a logical address?

7. Which layer of the OSI model is associated with the logical address?

8. Which address is displayed as hexadecimal numbers?

9. Which address allows transport between networks?

10. Which address does every host on a LAN segment evaluate?

LAB 1.4 CONNECTION-ORIENTED VERSUS CONNECTIONLESS COMMUNICATIONS

1

Objectives

Protocols that reside at the Transport layer of the OSI model can be connection-oriented or connectionless. The type of transport is usually determined by the application being used. Some applications, such as e-mail, require connection-oriented transfer. Some, such as Internet gaming, are best used with connectionless transfer.

The objective of this lab is to make sure you understand the characteristics of connection-oriented and connectionless communications.

After completing this lab, you will be able to:

➤ Understand the differences between connection-oriented and connectionless communications

Materials Required

This lab requires the following:

➤ A pen or pencil

Estimated completion time: **15 minutes**

ACTIVITY

1. The first column of Table 1-3 contains terms relating to either connection-oriented or connectionless communications. Match these terms to their correct Transport method by adding either "connection-oriented" or "connectionless" in the second column of each row.

Table 1-3   Connection-oriented versus connectionless communications

Description	Transport Method
ACK	
Unreliable	
Regular mail is an example	
Reliable	
Datagram	
Return receipt for mail is an example	
Sessions	

Certification Objectives

Objectives for the CCNA exam:

➤ Describe connection-oriented network service and connectionless network service, and identify their key differences

Review Questions

1. Where do connection-oriented and connectionless communications fit into the OSI model?

2. What typically decides whether connection-oriented or connectionless communications are used during a data transfer?

3. Which type of communications (connection-oriented or connectionless) do you think is faster and why?

4. What is the benefit of using connection-oriented communications?

CHAPTER TWO

NETWORK 2 DEVICES

Labs included in this chapter

➤ Lab 2.1 Simulate a Network by Connecting a CSU/DSU, Router, Bridge, Three Hubs, and Nine Computers

➤ Lab 2.2 Understanding Various Device Functions

➤ Lab 2.3 Understanding the Difference Between Bridges and Switches

---

CCNA Exam Objectives	
Objective	**Lab**
Describe the advantages of LAN segmentation	2.1
Describe LAN segmentation using bridges	2.1, 2.2, 2.3
Describe LAN segmentation using routers	2.1, 2.2
Describe the benefits of network segmentation with bridges	2.1, 2.2, 2.3
Describe the benefits of network segmentation with routers	2.1, 2.2
Describe LAN segmentation using switches	2.2, 2.3
Describe the benefits of network segmentation with switches	2.2, 2.3

LAB 2.1 SIMULATE A NETWORK BY CONNECTING A CSU/DSU, ROUTER, BRIDGE, THREE HUBS, AND NINE COMPUTERS

Objectives

As networks grow and become more complex, various devices, such as hubs, bridges, and routers, may need to be added. It is important to know how devices interconnect and operate on a LAN and WAN. It is also important to understand how these devices affect network traffic.

The objective of this lab is to provide you with the opportunity to connect a network using various WAN and LAN hardware. Although this is just a simulation, it gives you insight into the hardware connections required in a LAN/WAN relationship and how various devices affect network operations.

Figure 2-1 shows the configuration you will attempt to duplicate. In this lab, you will connect a CSU/DSU to a router with a standard serial cable. The router will then be connected to two hubs via Ethernet ports. On one side of the router there will be two hubs separated by a bridge. There is an additional hub on the other side of the router. (You will simulate the nine workstations in Figure 2-1 with old NIC cards.)

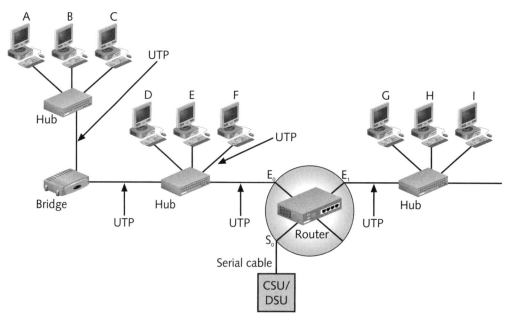

Figure 2-1   Network simulation setup

After completing this lab you will be able to:

➤ Identify various WAN and LAN devices

➤ Connect the WAN and LAN devices as shown in Figure 2-1

➤ Understand how various devices affect network communications

Materials Required

This lab requires the following:

➤ One CSU/DSU (may substitute a router if necessary)

➤ One Cisco router with two Ethernet ports and at least one serial port

➤ Transceivers for the router Ethernet ports if these Ethernet ports use an AUI connection instead of RJ-45

➤ Transceivers for the bridge connections if the bridge uses AUI connections instead of RJ-45

➤ Three hubs

➤ One bridge

➤ Nine NIC cards with RJ-45 transceivers for simulating the nine host computers in Figure 2-1

➤ Thirteen UTP patch cables

➤ One serial cable with a compatible connector for the serial interface on a router on one end and a v.35 connector on the other end to attach to the CSU/DSU. If another router is used instead of the CSU/DSU, the cable connector should match the serial interface on the additional router.

Estimated completion time: **30 minutes**

ACTIVITY

1. Lay out the devices on a table as shown in Figure 2-1.

2. Connect the CSU/DSU to a serial interface on the router using the serial cable.

3. Connect an Ethernet port on the router to a hub using UTP cable.

4. Connect the other Ethernet port on the router to another hub using UTP cable.

5. Connect the hub on the left to the bridge using UTP cable. There may be a toggle switch on the bridge that needs to be configured, depending on the type of cable you have connected to it. Make sure the switch is in the correct position.

6. Connect the bridge to the next hub using UTP cable.

7. Connect three patch cables to a hub using UTP patch cables. Make sure none of the patch cables are connected to the uplink port of the hub. The uplink port is used for hub-to-hub connections when using a straight-through patch cable instead of a crossover cable. You cannot use this port for workstations.

The uplink port is usually marked. Sometimes there is a switch that can be positioned to configure a regular port as an uplink port.

8. Now connect the other end of the patch cables used in Step 7 to the NICs to simulate connecting workstations.

9. Repeat Steps 7 and 8 for the other hubs and NICs to complete your simulated network.

Certification Objectives

Objectives for the CCNA exam:

➤ Describe the advantages of LAN segmentation

➤ Describe LAN segmentation using bridges

➤ Describe LAN segmentation using routers

➤ Describe the benefits of network segmentation with bridges

➤ Describe the benefits of network segmentation with routers

Review Questions

1. Which of the devices that you used in this lab are considered LAN equipment?

2. Which of the devices that you used in this lab are considered WAN equipment?

3. In Figure 2-1, are computers A, B, and C on the same network as D, E, and F?

4. In Figure 2-1, are computers A, B, and C on the same network as G, H, and I?

2

5. How does the bridge operate to filter traffic between the two attached segments in your network?

6. In Figure 2-1, how does the router operate to filter traffic between the segments off of E_0, E_1, and S_0?

7. What kind of domains do bridges create?

8. What kind of domains do routers create?

9. If the LANs in Figure 2-1 are 10 Mbps systems, which computers are sharing this bandwidth?

10. What kind of traffic is a bridge unable to filter?

LAB 2.2 UNDERSTANDING VARIOUS DEVICE FUNCTIONS

Objectives

It is important to understand how all devices operate on a network. These devices include repeaters, hubs, bridges, switches, brouters, routers, and gateways. The purpose of this lab is to make sure you understand the characteristics of all network devices.

After completing this lab you will be able to:

➤ Identify characteristics of repeaters, hubs, bridges, switches, brouters, routers, and gateways

Materials Required

This lab requires the following:

➤ A pen or pencil

Estimated completion time: **20 minutes**

ACTIVITY

1. Fill in the device column of Table 2-1 with the device being described. You can fill in the table with **repeater**, **hub**, **bridge**, **switch**, **brouter**, **router**, or **gateway**. Note that more than one device might be appropriate for a characteristic.

Table 2-1 Network device characteristics

Characteristic	Device(s)
Operates at upper layers to translate between different protocol suites	
Filters traffic based on MAC address	
Introduces the most latency on a network	
Boosts the signal, but does not segment the network	
Operates differently depending on whether nonroutable or routable protocols are in use	
Creates broadcast domains	
Creates a virtual circuit between sender and receiver	
Forwards broadcast traffic	
Filters traffic based on logical address	
Associated with the term "microsegmentation"	
Creates subnetworks	
Connects computers in a physical star and uses "shared bandwidth"	
Creates collision domains	
Operates at layer 1 of the OSI model	
Operates at layer 2 of the OSI model	
Operates at layer 3 of the OSI model	

Certification Objectives

Objectives for the CCNA exam:

➤ Describe LAN segmentation using bridges

➤ Describe LAN segmentation using routers

➤ Describe the benefits of network segmentation with bridges

➤ Describe the benefits of network segmentation with routers

➤ Describe LAN segmentation using switches

➤ Describe the benefits of network segmentation with switches

Review Questions

1. When is it appropriate to introduce a router into your network?

2. What can bridges do that hubs and repeaters cannot do?

3. When would introducing a brouter on your network be appropriate?

4. What are the advantages and disadvantages of using a gateway on your network?

5. What is the benefit of replacing hubs on your network with switches?

LAB 2.3 UNDERSTANDING THE DIFFERENCE BETWEEN BRIDGES AND SWITCHES

Objectives

Bridges and switches operate at the Data Link layer of the OSI model and filter traffic using the MAC address; however, they operate somewhat differently. The goal of this lab is for you to understand exactly how bridges and switches operate on a network. You will use Figures 2-2 and 2-3 to learn about properties of both bridges and switches.

After completing this lab you will be able to:

➤ Describe the tables bridges and switches used to filter traffic

➤ Explain why switches are the device of choice for enhancing network performance

Materials Required

This lab requires the following:

➤ A pen or pencil

Estimated completion time: **20 minutes**

ACTIVITY

1. Review Figure 2-2. In particular, note how the workstations, represented by letters, connect to the bridge.

2. Complete the bridging table shown in Figure 2-2 by filling in the columns in the table. Note that the letters in the figure represent MAC addresses on workstations.

3. Review Figure 2-3. In particular, note how the workstations, represented by letters, connect to the switch.

4. Complete the switching table shown in Figure 2-3 by filling in the columns in the table. The letters in the figure represent MAC addresses on workstations.

Certification Objectives

Objectives for the CCNA exam:

➤ Describe LAN segmentation using bridges

➤ Describe the benefits of network segmentation with bridges

➤ Describe LAN segmentation using switches

➤ Describe the benefits of network segmentation with switches

2

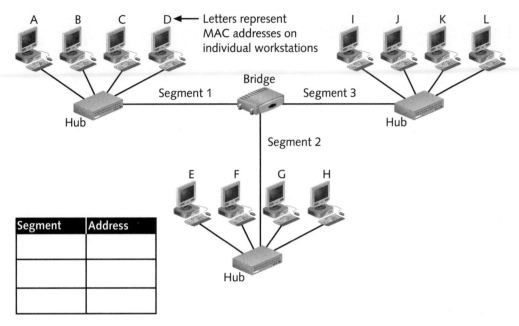

Segment	Address

Figure 2-2   Bridge with bridging table

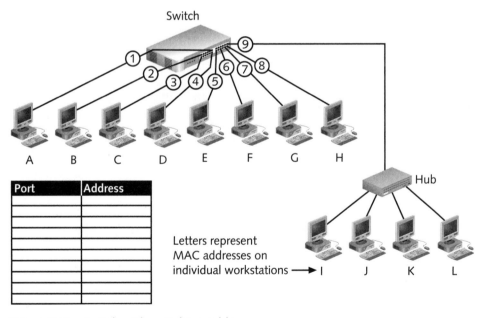

Port	Address

Figure 2-3   Switch with switching table

Review Questions

1. How many collision domains are defined in Figure 2-2?

2. How many collision domains are defined in Figure 2-3?

3. Examine Figure 2-2. If a frame from computer A has a destination MAC for computer D, which devices will see the layer 2 information?

4. Examine Figure 2-3. If a frame from computer A has a destination MAC for computer D, which devices will see the layer 2 information?

5. Examine Figure 2-3. In terms of network performance, what is the difference between computers A through H and I through L?

6. What will a bridge and switch do with a frame for which it has no information about the destination in its table?

7. How do bridges and switches handle broadcast frames?

8. Why is a switch considered more effective than a bridge in terms of increasing network performance?

9. In general, how do bridges and switches dynamically create their tables?

10. What happens to tables when bridges and switches are turned off?

TCP AND IP ADDRESSING

Labs included in this chapter

➤ Lab 3.1 Determine an IP Addressing Scheme for Network 192.3.2.0

➤ Lab 3.2 Decode the IP Address 172.16.31.255 /20

➤ Lab 3.3 Decode the IP Address 120.15.179.255 /18

➤ Lab 3.4 Design an Efficient IP Addressing Scheme for Network 176.10.0.0

➤ Lab 3.5 Determine IP and MAC Header Information in an ARP Request and ARP Reply

➤ Lab 3.6 Determine IP and MAC Header Information in a RARP Request

➤ Lab 3.7 Determine IP and MAC Header Information for a Data Packet

CCNA Exam Objectives	
Objective	Lab
Describe the two parts of network addressing; then identify the parts in specific protocol address examples	3.1, 3.2, 3.3, 3.4
Identify the parts in specific protocol address examples	3.1, 3.2, 3.3, 3.4
Describe the different classes of IP addresses (and subnetting)	3.1, 3.2, 3.3, 3.4

LAB 3.1 DETERMINE AN IP ADDRESSING SCHEME FOR NETWORK 192.3.2.0

Objectives

The objective of this lab is to demonstrate a logical way of determining an IP addressing scheme for the network shown in Figure 3-1. In this lab, you determine the subnet mask, the multiplier and usable subnetwork addresses, and the broadcast, interface, and host addresses. You will add labels to Figure 3-1 as you determine specific information.

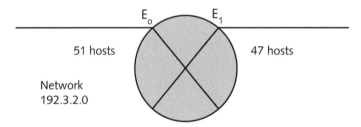

Figure 3-1   Example network

After completing this lab you will be able to:

➤ Determine the minimum number of bits to borrow when subnetting a given network

➤ Determine and assign IP addresses to the router interfaces and the hosts

➤ Understand which IP addresses are reserved and why

Materials Required

This lab requires the following:

➤ A pen or pencil

Estimated completion time: **20 minutes**

ACTIVITY

1. Review Figure 3-1. In particular, note the number of networks and the structure of the network number.

2. Determine the class of the network by examining the first octet of the network number given.

3. Notice that there are two interfaces, E_0 and E_1. How many usable subnets do you need?

_____

4. Use the formula $2^y-2=\#$ of usable subnetworks, to solve for y, where $y =$ the number of bits borrowed. Borrow just enough to cover the number of subnets you determined in Step 3.

_____

5. Use the formula $2^x-2=\#$ of usable host addresses (where x is the number of bits remaining in the host portion after borrowing) to make sure you have enough bits available for the hosts shown in Figure 3-1.

_____

6. Write the subnet mask in dotted decimal and in binary notation.

_____

7. Determine the multiplier by looking at the decimal value of the last bit borrowed as you move from left to right. The multiplier is either 128, 64, 32, 16, 8, 4, 2, or 1.

_____

8. Use the multiplier determined in Step 7 to determine the usable subnetwork addresses. The subnetwork addresses will increment by the value of the multiplier. Incrementing occurs in the octet in which borrowing broke off (the octet where the multiplier was determined).

_____

9. The last address on any subnet is always a broadcast address. Find this last possible IP address for each subnet. What are the broadcast addresses?

_____

10. Use the remaining addresses (all available addresses minus the subnet addresses and the broadcast addresses) for hosts. What is the range of hosts on each subnet?

_____

_____

_____

11. Assign the first host IP address in each subnet address to a router interface. This first address is available for hosts, but is traditionally used for the router interface connected to the subnet. What addresses did you assign?

_____

12. Write the subnet addresses in binary. How many bits are in the host portion? What does the host portion of these addresses look like?

_____

_____

13. Write the broadcast addresses in binary. What does the host portion of these addresses look like?

_____

Certification Objectives

Objectives for the CCNA exam:

➤ Describe the two parts of network addressing; then identify the parts in specific protocol address examples

➤ Identify the parts in specific protocol address examples

➤ Describe the different classes of IP addresses (and subnetting)

Review Questions

1. When working with IP addresses and subnetting, why is it important to first identify the class of address and the default subnet mask for that class?

2. What values can a multiplier be?

3. How do you find the multiplier?

4. Why must you subtract 2 from 2^y when determining the number of usable subnets?

5. Why must you subtract 2 from 2^x when determining the number of hosts per subnet?

6. How do you know where to begin incrementing when determining subnet numbers?

7. When working with IP addresses, which addresses can never be assigned to a host?

8. How can you tell an IP address is a network or subnetwork number if you write out the address in binary?

9. How can you tell that an IP address is a broadcast address if you write out the address in binary?

10. Must router interfaces be assigned the first available host address in a range?

LAB 3.2 DECODE THE IP ADDRESS 172.16.31.255 /20

Objectives

The objective of this lab is to help you become more familiar with subnetting and also to expose you to the bit-count notation used to express the subnet mask. Instead of writing out the subnet mask in dotted decimal notation, the bit-count method simply uses a forward slash followed by the number of consecutive ones in the mask. In this lab you will decode the IP address 172.16.31.255 /20 and determine the subnet mask, the multiplier, the network number, and the usable subnetwork addresses and broadcast addresses.

After completing this lab you will be able to:

➤ Recognize the subnet mask of an IP address given in bit-count format

➤ Determine the network number

➤ Determine subnetwork numbers and broadcast addresses

➤ Identify whether a given IP address is a broadcast, network, or host address

➤ Identify which subnetwork a given IP address is on

Materials Required

This lab requires the following:

➤ A pen or pencil

Estimated completion time: **20 minutes**

ACTIVITY

1. Determine the class of the network address given by examining the first octet.

_____

2. Determine the subnet mask by writing 1s for the first 20 bits of the address and 0s for the last 12 bits. How would you write this subnet mask in dotted decimal notation? How many bits have been borrowed?

_____

_____

_____

3. Use the formula 2^y-2 (where y is the number of bits borrowed from the default host portion) to calculate how many usable subnetworks can be created.

_____

4. Use the formula 2^x-2 (where x is the number of bits remaining in the host portion) to calculate how many usable hosts per subnetwork can be created.

_____

5. Determine the multiplier by looking at the decimal value of the last bit borrowed as you move from left to right. The multiplier is either 128, 64, 32, 16, 8, 4, 2, or 1.

_____

6. Determine the major network number in dotted decimal notation by substituting 0s for the default host portion of the given IP address.

_____

3

7. Use the multiplier determined in Step 5 to increment up through the first five usable subnetwork addresses. Incrementing occurs in the octet in which borrowing broke off.

_____

_____

_____

8. Determine the broadcast addresses on the five subnetworks listed in Step 7. The broadcast address on each subnetwork is the last possible address before the next subnet begins.

_____

_____

_____

9. What does the address 172.16.31.255 /20 represent?

_____

10. On what network is the given address in Step 9?

_____

Certification Objectives

Objectives for the CCNA exam:

➤ Describe the two parts of network addressing; then identify the parts in specific protocol address examples

➤ Identify the parts in specific protocol address examples

➤ Describe the different classes of IP addresses (and subnetting)

Review Questions

1. Where do you think the term "bit-count" comes from?

2. What is a benefit of using bit-count notation to express the subnet mask?

3. What would the bit-count notation of the IP address given in this lab have been if there were no subnetting?

4. If there were no subnetting in this lab, what would the given IP address have represented?

LAB 3.3 DECODE THE IP ADDRESS 120.15.179.255 /18

Objectives

The objective of this lab is to help you become familiar with subnetting and also the bit-count notation used to express the subnet mask. In this lab you will decode the IP address 120.15.179.255 /18 and determine the subnet mask, the multiplier, the network number, and usable subnetwork addresses and broadcast addresses.

After completing this lab you will be able to:

➤ Recognize the subnet mask of an IP address given in bit-count format

➤ Determine the network number

➤ Determine subnetwork numbers and broadcast addresses

➤ Identify whether a given IP address is a broadcast, network, or host address

➤ Identify which subnetwork a given IP address is on

Materials Required

This lab requires the following:

➤ A pen or pencil

Estimated completion time: **20 minutes**

ACTIVITY

1. Determine the class of the network by examining the first octet of the network address given. What is the default mask?

2. Determine the subnet mask by writing 1s for the first 18 bits of the address and 0s for the last 14 bits. How would you write this subnet mask in dotted decimal notation?

3

_____

3. Use the formula $2^y - 2$ (where y is the number of bits borrowed from the default host portion) to calculate how many usable subnetworks can be created.

_____

4. Use the formula $2^x - 2$ (where x is the number of bits remaining in the host portion) to calculate how many usable hosts per subnetwork can be created.

_____

5. Determine the multiplier by looking at the decimal value of the last bit borrowed as you move from left to right. The multiplier is either 128, 64, 32, 16, 8, 4, 2, or 1.

_____

6. Determine the major network number in dotted decimal notation by substituting 0s for the default host portion of the given IP address.

_____

7. Use the multiplier determined in Step 5 to determine the first six usable subnetwork addresses. The incrementing occurs in the octet in which borrowing broke off.

_____

8. Determine the broadcast addresses on the usable subnetworks listed in Step 7. The broadcast address on each subnetwork is the last possible address before the next subnet begins.

_____

9. What does the address 120.15.179.255 /18 represent?

_____

10. On what network is the IP address given in Step 9?

_____

Certification Objectives

Objectives for the CCNA exam:

➤ Describe the two parts of network addressing; then identify the parts in specific protocol address examples

➤ Identify the parts in specific protocol address examples

➤ Describe the different classes of IP addresses (and subnetting)

Review Questions

1. What makes subnetting with Class A and Class B addresses more difficult than subnetting with Class C addresses?

2. What is the maximum number of bits that can be borrowed with a Class C address?

3. What is the maximum number of bits that can be borrowed with a Class B address?

4. What is the maximum number of bits that can be borrowed with a Class A address?

5. What would the subnet mask be in dotted decimal notation for a Class C address if there were 30 hosts per subnet?

LAB 3.4 DESIGN AN EFFICIENT IP ADDRESSING SCHEME FOR NETWORK 176.10.0.0

Objectives

The objective of this lab is to give you a chance to use the subnetting formulas demonstrated in Labs 3.1 through 3.3 and to do so without as much guidance. Use what you have learned to logically determine an efficient IP addressing scheme for network 176.10.0.0, shown in Figure 3-2, and that allows 100% growth in the subnets.

3

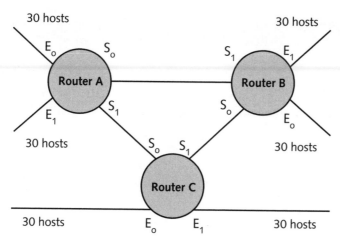

Figure 3-2 Network number 176.10.0.0

In this lab you will determine the subnet mask, the multiplier and usable subnetwork addresses, and the broadcast, interface, and host addresses. You will add labels to Figure 3-2 as you determine specific information.

 The "S_0" and "S_1" in Figure 3-2 represent serial links. Even though there are no hosts on these connections, they must be considered a subnet and the serial interfaces must be given IP addresses.

After completing this lab you will be able to:

➤ Determine the minimum number of bits to borrow when subnetting a given network and allowing for 100% growth

➤ Determine and assign IP addresses to the router interfaces and the hosts

➤ Determine the subnet addresses and broadcast addresses on each subnet

Materials Required

This lab requires the following:

➤ A pen or pencil

Estimated completion time: **20 minutes**

 ## ACTIVITY

1. Determine the class of the network by examining the first octet of the network address given.

2. Determine the number of subnets in Figure 3-2, and increase this number by 100% to allow for growth. For how many subnets do you allow?

_____

3. Determine how many bits must be borrowed in order to accommodate the number calculated in Step 2. How many usable subnets are available?

_____

4. Determine if borrowing the number of bits calculated in Step 3 leaves enough bits to accommodate the number of hosts per subnet indicated in Figure 3-2. How many usable hosts per subnetwork are available?

_____

5. Determine the new subnet mask in dotted decimal and in binary notation.

_____

6. Determine the subnet numbers of the nine existing subnets.

_____

_____

_____

_____

_____

7. Determine the broadcast addresses on each of the nine existing subnets.

_____

_____

_____

_____

_____

8. Determine the usable range of host addresses on each of the nine existing subnets.

_____

_____

_____

_____

_____

9. Assign IP addresses to the router interfaces below:
   - Router A: E_0, E_1, S_0, and S_1

   _____

   _____

   - Router B: E_0, E_1, S_0, and S_1

   _____

   _____

   - Router C: E_0, E_1, S_0, and S_1

   _____

   _____

10. Prove that 176.10.24.0 is a subnet number by using binary notation.

   _____

   _____

Certification Objectives

Objectives for the CCNA exam:

➤ Describe the two parts of network addressing; then identify the parts in specific protocol address examples

➤ Identify the parts in specific protocol address examples

➤ Describe the different classes of IP addresses (and subnetting)

Review Questions

1. True or False: Interfaces attached by point-to-point links such as the one between Router A's S_0 and Router B's S_1 in Figure 3-2 are on the same network (or subnetwork).

2. What kind of IP address is indicated by all binary ones in the host portion?

3. What kind of IP address is indicated by all binary zeroes in the host portion?

4. In every subnet created, why are two IP addresses unusable?

5. What is the purpose of a subnet mask?

6. What might you do if, when you borrowed enough bits for subnet numbers, you were not left with enough bits for host numbers?

LAB 3.5 DETERMINE IP AND MAC HEADER INFORMATION IN AN ARP REQUEST AND ARP REPLY

Objectives

The objective of this lab is to help you understand the information contained in the IP and MAC header of an ARP request and ARP reply. In this lab you will determine this IP and MAC information for an ARP request being issued by Computer A to determine the MAC address of Computer C, as illustrated in Figure 3-3.

Computer A

I want to send a message
to Computer C, but I don't
know C's MAC address.
C's IP address is 193.19.20.36.

My MAC: 05:61:8c:01:05:12
   My IP: 193.19.20.45

Figure 3-3   Computer A

After completing this lab you will be able to:

➤ Determine the IP and MAC header for an ARP request, given the known addresses indicated in Figure 3-3

➤ Determine the IP and MAC header for an ARP reply, given the known addresses indicated in Figures 3-4 and 3-5

Materials Required

This lab requires the following:

➤ A pen or pencil

Estimated completion time: **10 minutes**

ACTIVITY

1. Record the destination and source IP addresses in the IP header in Figure 3-4.

2. Record the destination and source MAC addresses in the MAC header in Figure 3-4.

MAC header		IP header		ARP request
Dest	Source	Dest	Source	What is your MAC address?

Figure 3-4   ARP request frame

3. Examine Figure 3-5. Then, record the destination and source IP addresses in the IP header in Figure 3-6.

4. Record the destination and source MAC addresses in the MAC header in Figure 3-6.

Computer C

I'm the one you're looking for.
My MAC address is
09:01:02:98:91:80.

Figure 3-5   Computer C

MAC header		IP header		ARP reply
Dest	Source	Dest	Source	Here is my MAC address.

Figure 3-6   ARP reply frame

Certification Objectives

Objectives for the CCNA exam:

This lab does not map to a certification objective; however, it contains information that is beneficial to your professional development

Review Questions

1. Explain your destination MAC address entry in Figure 3-4.

2. What will all hosts that see an ARP request do with the information?

3. How does a sending computer know a destination computer's IP address?

4. What type of frame is the ARP reply—unicast or broadcast?

5. Because ARP uses bandwidth by broadcasting, exactly how does ARP save bandwidth overall?

LAB 3.6 DETERMINE IP AND MAC HEADER INFORMATION IN A RARP REQUEST

Objectives

The objective of this lab is to help you understand the information contained in the IP and MAC header of a Reverse ARP (RARP) request. In this lab you will determine this IP and MAC information for the RARP request issued by Computer D, as shown in Figure 3-7.

Computer D

I know my MAC address is 01:09:42:71:93:64, but I don't know my IP address.

Figure 3-7   Computer D

After completing this lab you will be able to:

➤ Determine the IP and MAC header for a RARP request, given the known MAC address indicated in Figure 3-7

Materials Required

This lab requires the following:

➤ A pen or pencil

Estimated completion time: **10 minutes**

ACTIVITY

1. Examine Figure 3-7. Then, record the destination and source IP addresses in Figure 3-8 using the information in Figure 3-7.

2. Record the destination and source MAC addresses in Figure 3-8.

MAC header		IP header		RARP request
Dest	Source	Dest	Source	What is my IP address?

Figure 3-8   RARP request frame

Certification Objectives

Objectives for the CCNA exam:

This lab does not map to a certification objective; however, it contains information that is beneficial to your professional development

Review Questions

1. What kind of address is the destination MAC address in a RARP request?

2. How does a computer know its own MAC address?

3. Based on your lab activity, explain your entry for the source IP address in the RARP request.

4. What kind of address is the destination IP address in a RARP request?

5. How does the RARP server know which IP address to assign to a RARP client?

LAB 3.7 DETERMINE IP AND MAC HEADER INFORMATION FOR A DATA PACKET

Objectives

The objective of this lab is to help you understand the information contained in the IP and MAC header of a data packet as it travels from the source to the destination host through a router. In this lab you will determine this IP and MAC information between computer A and router interface E_1 and again between router interface E_0 and computer B, as shown in Figure 3-9.

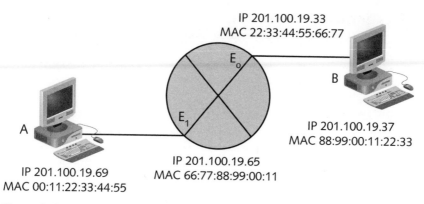

IP 201.100.19.33
MAC 22:33:44:55:66:77

B

IP 201.100.19.37
MAC 88:99:00:11:22:33

A

IP 201.100.19.65
MAC 66:77:88:99:00:11

IP 201.100.19.69
MAC 00:11:22:33:44:55

Figure 3-9   MAC and IP header information

After completing this lab you will be able to:

➤ Determine the IP and MAC header for a data packet as it travels through a router, given the known MAC and IP information indicated in Figure 3-9

➤ Understand the concept of a default gateway

Materials Required

This lab requires the following:

➤ A pen or pencil

Estimated completion time: **10 minutes**

ACTIVITY

1. Record the destination and source IP addresses in Figure 3-10 for a frame transmitted from computer A to interface E_1 on the router that is destined for computer B.

MAC header		IP header		Data
Dest	Source	Dest	Source	

Figure 3-10   Frame from computer A to router interface E_1

2. Record the destination and source MAC address in Figure 3-10 for a frame transmitted from computer A to interface E_1 on the router that is destined for computer B.

3. Record the destination and source IP addresses in Figure 3-11 for a frame transmitted from the E_0 interface on the router to computer B during its journey from computer A to computer B.

4. Record the destination and source MAC address in Figure 3-11 for a frame transmitted from E_0 on the router to computer B during its journey from computer A to computer B.

MAC header		IP header		Data
Dest	Source	Dest	Source	

Figure 3-11   Frame from router interface E_0 to computer B

Certification Objectives

Objectives for the CCNA exam:

This lab does not map to a certification objective; however, it contains information that is beneficial to your professional development

Review Questions

1. In Figure 3-9, what is the default gateway for computer A?

2. In Figure 3-9, what is the default gateway for computer B?

3. What can you say about the source and destination IP addresses in a frame as the data travels across routers in its journey from original sender to ultimate receiver?

4. What can you say about the source and destination MAC addresses in a frame as the data travels across routers in its journey from original sender to ultimate receiver?

5. Where do routers get the information necessary to make forwarding decisions?

6. Why do computers usually need a default gateway, and when is it used?

CHAPTER FOUR

NETWORK TOPOLOGY AND DESIGN

Labs included in this chapter

➤ Lab 4.1 Make and Test a Straight-through Patch Cable

➤ Lab 4.2 Make and Test a Crossover Patch Cable

➤ Lab 4.3 Identify Various Cable Types and Connectors

➤ Lab 4.4 Punch Down and Test UTP Cable

➤ Lab 4.5 Calculate Bandwidth

CCNA Exam Objectives

These labs do not map to certification objectives; however, they contain information that will be beneficial to your professional development.

LAB 4.1 MAKE AND TEST A STRAIGHT-THROUGH PATCH CABLE

Objectives

The objective of this lab is to teach you to make a typical unshielded twisted-pair (UTP) patch cable. Although you can readily purchase patch cables, making and testing one will give you insight to how UTP cable is made and how it operates. In addition, there are some instances where you will have to make a cable, so it is important to know how.

In this lab you will make a straight-through cable per the EIA/TIA 568B specifications shown in Figure 4-1. You will then test the cable using a simple continuity tester or other cable tester.

EIA/TIA 568B Ethernet-data	White/ orange	Orange	White/ green	Blue	White/ blue	Green	White/ brown	Brown
EIA/TIA 568A voice & data	White/ green	Green	White/ orange	Blue	White/ blue	Orange	White/ brown	Brown

Figure 4-1   EIA/TIA patch cable specifications

After completing this lab you will be able to:

➤ Make a working patch cable per EIA/TIA 568B specifications

➤ Test the cable for continuity

Materials Required

This lab requires the following:

➤ A box or spool of Cat 5 UTP cable

➤ One UTP cable crimper and one pair of wire cutters for every four students

➤ Box of RJ-45 connectors

➤ One UTP continuity tester (or other cable tester) for every four students

Estimated completion time: **60 minutes**

ACTIVITY

1. Score (do not penetrate) the jacket of the cable with the wire cutters at about 1.5" down. Remove the outer jacket only, not the insulation on the individual wires.

2. Bend the cable gently at the score mark and try to snap off the jacket.

3. Untwist all the wires down to the jacket.

4. Moving from left to right, put the wires in order. Use the EIA/TIA 568B standard colors shown in Figure 4-1.

5. Use your thumb and finger to flatten the wires.

6. Hold the wires flat and tightly together with the thumb and finger of one hand, close to the base of the jacket.

7. Use the wire cutters to snip the wires all at once in a straight line to about 0.5" above the base of the jacket.

8. Keep your grip on the wires while you slide the RJ-45 connector onto the ends of the wires. Make sure you still have the wires in the correct order. The clip of the connector should be face down.

9. Slide the wires all the way in, and make sure the edge of the jacket slides just up under the edge of the connector about 0.25".

10. Slip the connector into the crimper tool. The clip of the connector should be face down.

11. Keep your hands free of the blade as you squeeze the handles of the tool together until they release again.

12. Repeat Steps 1 through 11 for the other end of the wire. Use the same EIA/TIA 568B standard for this opposite end.

13. Now test your cable by inserting both ends of the cable into the continuity tester. As you continually press the tester button, the indicator lights should light up to tell you that you have a good connection for each of the eight connections. If you have a more advanced type of tester, you may use that instead.

    The lights should match if you made a successful, straight-through EIA/TIA cable; that is, light one on the left side should match up with light one on the right side. If light one matches up with light two, for example, you have crossed pairs.

14. If your cables fail the test, visually inspect the connector and make sure the color coding is correct.

15. If the color coding is correct and the cable is still failing, try re-crimping the connectors.

16. If the color coding is incorrect or re-crimping doesn't work, you have to cut the wire and start over. You cannot reuse the connector after it has been crimped.

Certification Objectives

Objectives for the CCNA exam:

This lab does not map to a certification objective; however, it contains information that is beneficial to your professional development.

Review Questions

1. When might you have to make a patch cable?

2. What does a wire map tell you?

3. Why is it important to slide the jacket of the cable under the connector?

4. What kind of interference results from the bleeding of the signal from one wire pair onto another?

5. What are the two most popular LAN architectures using UTP?

LAB 4.2 MAKE AND TEST A CROSSOVER PATCH CABLE

Objectives

The objective of this lab is to teach you to make a crossover UTP patch cable. A crossover cable may be required when connecting a hub to a hub or other device-to-device connection. A crossover cable is also known as a cross-connect cable.

Although you can readily purchase crossover cables, making and testing one will give you insight about how UTP cable is made and how a crossover cable differs from a straight-through cable. In addition, you may find yourself in the position of having to make a crossover cable, so it is important that you know how.

In this lab you will make a crossover cable per the EIA/TIA 568A and 568B specifications shown in Figure 4-1. You will then test the cable using a simple continuity tester.

After completing this lab you will be able to:

➤ Make a working crossover cable per EIA/TIA 568A and 568B specifications

➤ Test the cable for continuity

Materials Required

This lab requires the following:

➤ A box or spool of Cat 5 UTP cable

➤ One UTP cable crimper and one pair of wire cutters for every four students

➤ Box of RJ-45 connectors

➤ One UTP continuity tester (or other cable tester) for every four students

4

Estimated completion time: **60 minutes**

ACTIVITY

1. Score (do not penetrate) the jacket of the cable with the wire cutters at about 1.5" down. Remove the outer jacket only, not the insulation on the individual wires.

2. Bend the cable gently at the score mark and try to snap off the jacket.

3. Untwist all the wires down to the jacket.

4. Moving from left to right, put the wires in order. Use the EIA/TIA 568B standard colors shown in Figure 4-1.

5. Use your thumb and third finger to flatten the wires.

6. Hold the wires flat and tightly together with the thumb and third finger of one hand, close to the base.

7. Use the wire cutters to snip the wires to about 0.5" above the base of the jacket.

8. Keep your grip on the wires while you slide the RJ-45 connector onto the ends of the wires. Make sure you still have the wires in the correct order. The clip of the connector should be face down.

9. Slide the wires all the way in, and make sure the edge of the jacket slides just up under the edge of the connector about 0.25".

10. Slip the connector into the crimper tool. The clip of the connector should be face down.

11. Keep your hands free of the blade as you squeeze the handles of the tool together until they release again.

12. Repeat Steps 1 through 11 for the other end of the wire, but this time use the color configuration that corresponds to the EIA/TIA 568A standard in Figure 4-1. This will make the cable a crossover cable. Visually inspect your cable.

13. Now test your cable by inserting both ends of the cable into the tester. As you continually press the tester button, the indicator lights should light up to tell you that you have a good connection for each of the eight connections.

If you made a successful crossover cable, the lights for one and three should match and the lights for two and six should match, as shown in Figure 4-2.

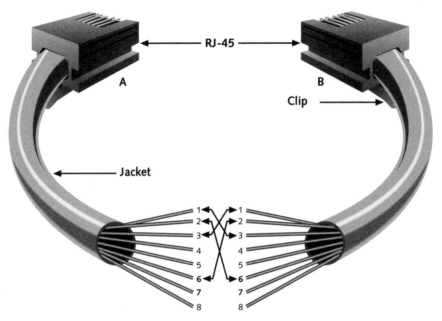

Figure 4-2   Crossover cable

14. If your cables fail the test, visually inspect the connector and make sure the color coding is correct.

15. If the color coding is correct and the cable still fails, try re-crimping the connectors.

16. If the color coding is not correct or re-crimping doesn't work, you will have to cut the wire and start over. You cannot reuse the connector after it has been crimped.

Certification Objectives

Objectives for the CCNA exam:

This lab does not map to a certification objective; however, it contains information that will be beneficial to your professional development.

Review Questions

1. In a UTP cable, which wires does Ethernet use?

2. When might you need a crossover cable?

3. If you have made a successful crossover cable, what does the wire map indicate?

4. What organizations control the specifications for UTP cable configuration on Ethernet networks?

5. What kind of tool is used to connect the RJ-45 connector to the wires when making a patch cable?

4

LAB 4.3 IDENTIFY VARIOUS CABLE TYPES AND CONNECTORS

Objectives

The objective of this lab is to help you become familiar with various cable types and connectors that might be part of a LAN or WAN. In this lab, your instructor will label examples of cable and connectors with the letters A through K. You will match the labeled hardware with the descriptions below.

After completing this lab you will be able to:

➤ Identify various cable types and connectors that are part of typical LAN/WAN installations

Materials Required

This lab requires the following:

➤ Examples of cable and connectors, as listed in the Activity section in this lab, that are labeled from A through K

Estimated completion time: **30 minutes**

ACTIVITY

1. Match the labeled connectors and cable with the descriptions below. Put the letter associated with the description next to it.

- Thinnet   _____
- Thicknet   _____
- Category 5 UTP   _____
- Category 3 UTP   _____
- Multimode fiber   _____
- Single-mode fiber   _____
- STP   _____
- T-connector   _____
- RJ-45 connector   _____
- RG-58 terminator   _____
- Plenum cable   _____

Certification Objectives

Objectives for the CCNA exam:

This lab does not map to a certification objective; however, it contains information that will be beneficial to your professional development.

Review Questions

1. What is the difference between multimode and single-mode fiber?

2. What purpose does the RG-58 terminator serve?

3. What is the difference between STP and UTP?

4. What is the difference between Category 3 and Category 5 UTP?

5. Why don't you see thinnet or thicknet in use on LANs much anymore?

4

Lab 4.4 Punch Down and Test UTP Cable

Objectives

The purpose of this lab is to familiarize you with a patch panel and to teach you to punch down and test cable.

In this lab you will use the EIA/TIA 568B specification to make one end of a patch cable. You will connect the other end to the pin side of the patch panel using the proper technique. You will finish by testing your connection for continuity.

After completing this lab you will be able to:

➤ Punch down UTP cable into a patch panel

➤ Test the connection using a simple cable tester

Materials Required

This lab requires the following:

➤ One patch panel for every four students, preferably mounted on a rack to hold it steady

➤ One Krone tool or other punch-down tool for every four students

➤ Spool of Category 5 UTP cable

➤ A box of RJ-45 connectors

➤ One pair of wire cutters for every four students

➤ Several properly made UTP patch cables for testing

Estimated completion time: **60 minutes**

Activity

1. Make one end of an EIA/TIA 568B patch cable following the specifications in Figure 4-1.

2. At the opposite end of the cable connection you just made, score (do not penetrate) the jacket of the cable with the wire cutters at about 1.5" down. Remove the outer jacket only, not the insulation on the individual wires.

3. Bend the cable gently at the score mark and try to snap off the jacket.

4. Untwist the wires as little as possible.

5. Moving from left to right, line up wire colors with the punch-down block pin colors. The striped wires go to the left of the pin; the solid color wires go to the right of the pin.

6. Push the wires between the pins, being careful to keep the correct color order. Only 0.25" of wire should be exposed between the cable jacket and the pins. Let the rest of the wire stick out above the pins.

7. Keep the cable centered about the pins. If the cable becomes skewed to the right or left, network performance will be affected.

8. Position the punch-down tool over the first wire. The cut side of the tool should face up.

9. Position the tool perpendicular to the block. Push into the wire with the tool.

10. The excess wire above the block should snap off. If it doesn't, you can twist it off with your fingers.

11. Continue punching down the rest of the wires.

12. When you finish, you should have a UTP cable attached at one end to the punch-down block. An RJ-45 connector should be at the other end.

13. To test the continuity of the connection, connect a regular EIA/TIA 568B patch cable to the port on the other side of the punch-down block that corresponds to the pin you have wired.

14. Plug the end of the patch cable that is connected to the port into a cable tester.

15. Plug the patch cable that is connected to the pin side of the block into the cable tester.

16. Each time you press the test button, the indicator lights should tell you that you have a good connection for that particular pair of wires.

17. If your cables fail the test, start troubleshooting with the help of your instructor.

Certification Objectives

Objectives for the CCNA exam:

This lab does not map to a certification objective; however, it contains information that will be beneficial to your professional development.

Review Questions

1. True or False? You should follow the color coding on the pins rather than the EIA/TIA 568A or 568B standard.

2. What is the opposite side of the pin side of the panel called?

3. What is the purpose of a patch panel?

4. What is the name of the tool used when attaching UTP cable wires to the pin side of the panel?

5. Does a patch panel repeat a signal?

LAB 4.5 CALCULATE BANDWIDTH

Objectives

The objective of this lab is to practice bandwidth and throughput calculations. Before you can design the topology of the network, you must discover the maximum bandwidth that will be demanded on the network. You should then factor in a growth allowance.

For the most part, bandwidth determines the media type, and the media type in turn dictates the physical and logical network topology. In this lab you will determine the bandwidth required for a hypothetical network based on the parameters given. You will then determine the type of topology that this bandwidth dictates.

After completing this lab you will be able to:

➤ Calculate bandwidth given file size and transmission time

➤ Understand how and why bandwidth determines topology

Materials Required

This lab requires the following:

➤ Pencil or pen

➤ Calculator

Estimated completion time: **30 minutes**

ACTIVITY

1. Review the scenario below.

   Lowry A/V, Inc., is an emerging e-commerce and call center based in Charlottesville, Virginia, that sells and distributes high-end audio and video equipment via the Web and catalogs. Recently, they decided to build an additional facility in Malabar, Florida. This expansion requires a complete redesign of the company's network. On the LAN side they need to back up their database twice a day. The company's database is typically about 5 GB in size, but may increase over the next few years. This backup should not take more than 10 minutes. On the WAN side, the firm needs approximately 1.2 Mbps.

2. What formula do you use to calculate the necessary bandwidth for the LAN?

3. What is the LAN bandwidth required in Mbps? Do not adjust for growth at this time.

4. If the company wants a 40% growth factor built into the calculation, what will the new bandwidth requirement be?

5. Which cable type would you recommend for the LAN? Justify your answer.

6. Lowry A/V is considering a T1 connection for the WAN. Use the bandwidth formula to determine approximately how fast in seconds they will be able to transmit a 6 MB file across the T1 link. The bandwidth of a T1 is 1.54 Mbps.

Certification Objectives

Objectives for the CCNA exam:

This lab does not map to a certification objective; however, it contains information that will be beneficial to your professional development.

Review Questions

1. What is the difference between throughput and bandwidth?

2. What is the purpose of the growth factor?

4

3. What cable types, other than UTP, can be used on a LAN?

4. What are the benefits of using UTP?

CHAPTER FIVE

WAN CONCEPTS

Labs included in this chapter

➤ Lab 5.1 Identify Connection Methods Used with WAN Data Link Layer Protocols

➤ Lab 5.2 Understand WAN Switching Terminology

➤ Lab 5.3 Associate WAN Technologies with the Appropriate Layer of the OSI Reference Model

CCNA Exam Objectives	
Objective	**Lab**
Recognize key Frame Relay terms and features.	5.1, 5.2, 5.3
Identify ISDN protocols, function groups, reference points, and channels.	5.1, 5.2, 5.3

LAB 5.1 IDENTIFY CONNECTION METHODS USED WITH WAN DATA LINK LAYER PROTOCOLS

Objectives

The objective of this lab is to clarify the relationship between WAN Data Link layer protocols and the connection methods with which they are typically used. In this lab you will define the protocol acronyms and indicate whether a particular WAN Data Link layer protocol is associated with point-to-point, multipoint, or switched connection methods.

After completing this lab you will:

➤ Understand the three connection methods used in WAN transmission

➤ Understand the various Data Link layer protocols associated with the WAN connection methods

Materials Required

This lab requires the following:

➤ Pencil or pen

Estimated completion time: **20 minutes**

ACTIVITY

1. For each protocol listed in Table 5-1, give the definition. Then, write in the WAN connection method—point-to-point, multipoint, or switched—that applies to each protocol. Note that a protocol can be associated with more than one connection method.

Table 5-1   WAN connection methods

WAN Protocol	Define the Acronym	Connection Method
LAPD		
SDLC		
PPP		
X.25		
ATM		
HDLC		
Frame Relay		

Certification Objectives

Objectives for the CCNA exam:

➤ Recognize key Frame Relay terms and features.

➤ Identify ISDN protocols, function groups, reference points, and channels.

Review Questions

1. Why might you choose a point-to-point dedicated line rather than a switched service?

2. What it is the advantage of Frame Relay as compared to X.25?

3. How is ATM different from X.25 and Frame Relay?

4. On which protocol is PPP based?

5. Which protocol did PPP replace?

LAB 5.2 UNDERSTAND WAN SWITCHING TERMINOLOGY

Objectives

The objective of this lab is to help you learn the terminology and definitions associated with switching technologies. In this lab, you will match the correct switching term with a definition.

After completing this lab you will:

➤ Understand characteristics of WAN switching technologies

➤ Relate WAN switching terms to the technology with which they are associated

Materials Required

This lab requires the following:

➤ Pencil or pen

Estimated completion time: **20 minutes**

ACTIVITY

1. Match each term in the following bulleted list with a definition in the numbered list.

- X.25
- LAPB
- Inverse ARP
- DLCI
- Frame Relay
- multiplex
- PVC
- CIR
- LMI
- ISDN
- BRI
- ATM

- BECN
- FECN
- D-channel
- B-channel
- X.21
- LAPD
- Cell
- CSU/DSU
- Synchronous
- Asynchronous
- Terminal adapter
- Packet-switched

2. Type of network in which relatively small units of data are routed through a network based on the destination address. The data units may take different paths to the destination.

_____

3. LAN and WAN protocol that handles digital data transmission up to 622 Mbps. Requires dedicated hardware.

_____

4. ITU standard for dial-up, digital transmission over ordinary telephone wires, in addition to other media. Transmission speeds are up to 128 Kbps for home use.

_____

5. Hardware that converts digital data frames from a LAN into frames appropriate for a WAN and vice versa. Provider end of the WAN link.

_____

6. Cost-efficient data transmission protocol that uses a variable-size packet and leaves any necessary error correction to the upper-layer protocols.

_____

7. ISDN service consisting of two, 64-Kbps B-channels and one, 16-Kbps D-channel.

_____

8. Keepalive mechanism for Frame Relay that periodically sends the router status information regarding a transmission.

   _____

9. Allows Frame Relay router to discover the destination address of a node associated with the virtual circuit.

   _____

10. Carries control and signaling information for ISDN.

   _____

11. Underlying Data Link layer protocol for X.25.

   _____

12. Used to identify the PVC or SVC on a Frame Relay network.

   _____

13. Minimum bandwidth associated with a logical connection in a Frame Relay network.

   _____

14. Term used for the fixed-length packet associated with ATM transmission.

   _____

15. Should result in a router transmitting less traffic.

   _____

16. Relies on start and stop bits to define end points of a transmission.

   _____

17. Physical layer standard that defines the interface between the DTE and the DCE.

   _____

18. Warns the next router that congestion has been experienced.

   _____

19. Underlying protocol for transmission over ISDN lines.

   _____

20. A Frame Relay connection that the network administrator sets up and that performs as if it were a dedicated line.

   _____

21. Used to transfer data over ISDN lines.

   _____

22. Combining different traffic streams onto a single physical line.

   _____

23. Interface between non-ISDN equipment and an ISDN line.

_____

24. Data Link layer WAN protocol originally developed to work over existing analog phone lines. Uses extensive error checking.

_____

25. Communications that rely on a clock.

_____

Certification Objectives

Objectives for the CCNA exam:

> ➤ Recognize key Frame Relay terms and features.
> ➤ Identify ISDN protocols, function groups, reference points, and channels.

Review Questions

1. List all the terms in this lab that relate to Frame Relay.

2. List all the terms in this lab that relate to ISDN.

3. What are the two ISDN services and their corresponding bandwidths?

LAB 5.3 WAN TECHNOLOGIES AND THE OSI REFERENCE MODEL

Objectives

The objective of this lab is to learn where WAN technologies fit into the OSI reference model. In this lab, you will indicate at which OSI layer or layers the listed WAN technology resides.

After completing this lab you will:

> ➤ Understand where various WAN technologies fit into the OSI reference model

Materials Required

This lab requires the following:

➤ Pencil or pen

➤ Computer with Internet access for help in answering the review questions

Estimated completion time: **20 minutes**

5

ACTIVITY

1. Next to each WAN technology listed in Table 5-2, write at which layer or layers of the OSI reference model the technology resides.

Table 5-2   WAN technologies in the OSI model

WAN Technology	Associated OSI Model Layer(s)
RS-232	
X.25	
LAPD	
HSSI	
Frame Relay	
SDLC	
X.21	
V.35	
PPP	
HDLC	
ATM	
EIA -530	

Certification Objectives

Objectives for the CCNA exam:

➤ Recognize key Frame Relay terms and features.

➤ Identify ISDN protocols, function groups, reference points, and channels.

Review Questions

1. Define the RS-232 specification. In particular, indicate the connector type and the supported bandwidth.

2. Define the EIA-530 specification. In particular, indicate the connector type and the bandwidth supported.

3. Define the HSSI specification. In particular, indicate the connector type and the bandwidth supported.

4. Define the V.35 specification. In particular, indicate the bandwidth supported.

5. Define the X.21 specification. In particular, indicate the bandwidth supported.

ROUTER AND IOS BASICS

Labs included in this chapter

➤ Lab 6.1 Connect the Internetwork Lab

➤ Lab 6.2 Configure HyperTerminal to Access a Cisco Router

➤ Lab 6.3 Use the System Configuration Dialog to Configure a Cisco Router

➤ Lab 6.4 Configure Console and Aux Passwords

➤ Lab 6.5 Use HELP, the Command History, Enhanced Editing Features, and the show Command

---

CCNA Exam Objectives	
Objective	Lab
Examine router elements	6.1, 6.5
Check an initial configuration using the setup command	6.3
Prepare the initial configuration of your router and enable IP	6.3
Manage configuration files from the privileged EXEC mode	6.4
Control router passwords, identification, and banner	6.4
Log in to a router in both user and privileged modes	6.4, 6.5
Use the context-sensitive Help facility	6.5
Use the command history and editing features	6.5
Identify the main Cisco IOS software commands for router startup	6.5

LAB 6.1 CONNECT THE INTERNETWORK LAB

Objectives

The objective of this lab is to give you experience in making the hardware connections necessary to configure the Cisco router lab. This includes connecting computers, hubs, and routers to each other. In this lab you will connect five Cisco routers, five hubs, and five computers in preparation for router configuration.

After completing this lab you will be able to:

➤ Identify routers, hubs, transceivers, DCE/DTE cables, rollover cables, DB9 and/or DB25 connectors, and the COM ports on the computers

➤ Correctly connect the hardware using the proper cables

Materials Required

This lab requires the following:

➤ Four 2501 series routers with power cables (could substitute a different series but must have two serial interfaces and one Ethernet interface)

➤ One 2514 series router with power cable (could substitute a different series but must have two serial interfaces and two Ethernet interfaces)

➤ Five hubs with power cables (can substitute switches)

➤ Three V.35 DTE cables (male) with serial ends to match serial interfaces on routers

➤ Three V.35 DCE cables (female) with serial ends to match serial interfaces on routers

➤ Six UTP patch cables

➤ Six Ethernet 10BaseT UTP-to-AUI transceivers (you will not need these if the Ethernet interfaces on the routers are RJ-45 transceivers)

➤ Five RJ-45 to RJ-45 rollover cables

➤ Five RJ-45 to DB-25 or DB-9 connectors

➤ Power strips

➤ Five Windows 98 (or other Windows operating system) computers with a COM port available. Computers should be set up and labeled lab-a through lab-e, as shown in Figure 6-1. It is OK if the routers and hubs are in a rack.

➤ Routers labeled lab-a through lab-e. Router A should be the router with the two Ethernet interfaces.

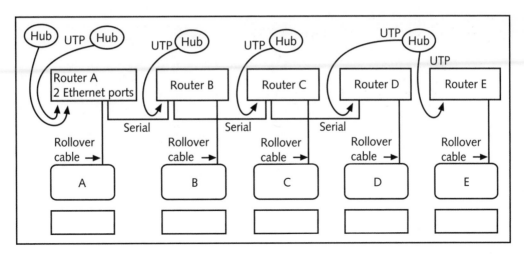

Figure 6-1   Standard internetwork lab configuration

6

Estimated completion time: **30 minutes**

ACTIVITY

1. Lay the five routers on the long table behind the computers with the routers' port sides facing the back of the computers. Alternatively, load the routers in a rack in order from the lab-a router at the top to the lab-e router at the bottom.

2. Place a hub behind or on top of each router.

3. Refer to Figure 6-2 for help with the next steps regarding cabling. The TFTP server will be connected in Lab 7.2.

4. Connect the lab-a router's first Ethernet interface to the hub behind it using a UTP patch cable. You may need a transceiver on the AUI0 port on the router to accept the RJ-45 connector. At the hub, make sure the UTP is not plugged into an uplink port. Ask your instructor for help if you cannot determine which port is the uplink port.

5. Connect the lab-a router to a second hub via its second Ethernet port or AUI1 port, as outlined in Step 4.

6. Connect the lab-b router to a third hub, as outlined in Step 4.

7. Connect the lab-c router to a fourth hub, as outlined in Step 4.

8. Connect both the lab-d and lab-e routers to the fifth hub, as outlined in Step 4 and shown in Figure 6-2.

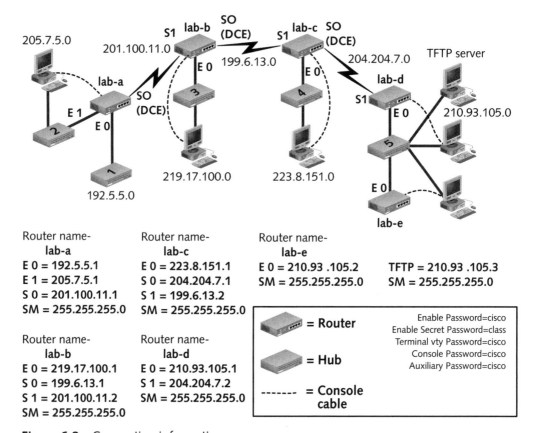

Figure 6-2 Connection information

9. Connect the console port of the lab-a router to a COM port on computer A using the router rollover cable and Figure 6-1 as your guide. At the COM port, you will need either a DB-25 or DB-9 connector between the RJ-45 rollover cable and the COM port.

10. Repeat Step 9 for the remaining routers and computers.

11. The DTE and DCE cables should be marked as such. Connect each V.35 end of a DTE cable to the V.35 end of a DCE cable. You should now have three cables, each with a DTE end and a DCE end.

12. The 60-pin ends (or other serial end types) of the DTE and DCE serial cables should be connected to the serial ports on the routers. Be extremely careful to line up the connections correctly. Pins can easily be damaged if a connection is forced. Connect the lab-a router to the lab-b router using Figure 6-2 as a reference. Notice that the DCE end goes in the lab-a router's S0 port, and the DTE end goes in the lab-b router's S1 port. In this lab setup, the DCE ends always go into the S0 ports.

13. Repeat Step 12 to connect the lab-b router to the lab-c router, and again to connect the lab-c router to the lab-d router.

14. Connect all devices to the power strips using the correct power cables.

15. Ask your instructor to check your lab setup.

Certification Objectives

Objectives for the CCNA exam:

➤ Examine router elements

Review Questions

1. For what is a transceiver used?

2. This lab connects routers directly to each other via serial cables. Is this a typical configuration? If not, to what equipment does the DCE end of the serial cable usually connect?

3. What does a rollover (console) cable look like?

4. What kind of port does the console cable attach to on the computer?

5. What kind of port does the UTP patch cable attach to on the router?

LAB 6.2 CONFIGURE HYPERTERMINAL TO ACCESS A CISCO ROUTER

Objectives

The objective of this lab is to give you experience configuring the Windows HyperTerminal program, which is frequently used to configure routers. In this lab you will configure HyperTerminal on a computer connected to a router via the console port. The computer was connected to the router in Lab 6.1.

After completing this lab you will be able to:

➤ Configure HyperTerminal on a Windows computer for use in configuring Cisco routers

Materials Required

This lab requires the following:

➤ The internetworking lab setup in Lab 6.1 and shown in Figure 6-2, or a Windows computer connected to a Cisco router via the console port on the router

➤ HyperTerminal installed on a Windows computer

Estimated completion time: **30 minutes**

ACTIVITY

1. Make sure the router connected to the computer is turned off.

2. Turn on the Windows computer.

3. Click **Start**, point to **Programs**, point to **Accessories**, point to **Communications**, and then click **HyperTerminal**. This is the procedure for a Windows 98 computer. The procedure for accessing HyperTerminal on other Windows operating systems may be slightly different.

4. Double-click the **Hypertrm** program to open the New Connection window.

5. Enter an area code if prompted, and then click **No** if asked to install a modem.

6. In the Connection Description dialog box, enter the name **Cisco** for the connection. Click **OK** to continue.

7. You must now configure your connection to the router via the Connect To dialog box. In the **Connect Using** selection box, choose the COM port to which the RJ-45 to DB-9 or DB-25 connector is attached. Click **OK** to continue.

8. Configure these settings for the COM port: Bits per second: **9600**; Data bits: **8**; Parity: **None**; Stop bits: **1**; Flow control: **Hardware**. Click **OK** to complete the configuration.

9. Click **File**, and then click **Save** to save the connection.

10. Close HyperTerminal, click **Yes** if prompted to confirm, and then double-click the connection to reopen it.

11. Turn on the connected router.

12. Watch for the router start-up information. You may need to press **Enter** on the computer keyboard to initiate this process.

13. When you know HyperTerminal is correctly configured, you may turn off the router and exit HyperTerminal and Windows or continue with the next lab.

Certification Objectives

Objectives for the CCNA exam:

This lab does not map to a certification objective; however, it contains information that is beneficial to your professional development.

Review Questions

1. What program on a Windows computer is used for configuring a Cisco router?

2. What are the important settings to configure in HyperTerminal to access a Cisco router?

3. Where is the HyperTerminal program located in Windows 98?

4. Which port on a router do you use to connect the rollover cable when configuring the router with HyperTerminal?

5. You can use the auxiliary port on a router to access it with HyperTerminal. How would you be accessing the router if you used this port?

LAB 6.3 USE THE SYSTEM CONFIGURATION DIALOG TO CONFIGURE A CISCO ROUTER

Objectives

The objective of this lab is to give you experience with the initial configuration of a Cisco router using the System Configuration Dialog. The System Configuration Dialog is a type of "wizard" in that you are prompted to enter the information that configures the router. This is easier than direct configuration using the command line.

Although most professionals do not use this method to configure Cisco routers, knowledge of the System Configuration Dialog is a CCNA objective. It is important to know how to use it and what it does. Remember that setting up the router using this method makes the router operational; however, it may not be completely configured.

After completing this lab you will be able to:

➤ Use the System Configuration Dialog to configure the routers in the internetworking lab shown in Figure 6-2

➤ Know how to access the System Configuration Dialog

➤ Understand the capabilities and limitations of the System Configuration Dialog

Materials Required

This lab requires the following:

➤ The internetworking lab setup, per Lab 6.2

➤ HyperTerminal configured to access the routers via the console port, per Lab 6.2

Estimated completion time: **45 minutes**

ACTIVITY

1. Refer to Figure 6.2. What will the hostname of your router be?

    _____

2. Which interfaces is your router using?

    _____

3. What are the IP addresses and subnet masks for those interfaces?

    _____

4. What is the enable secret password?

    _____

5. What is the enable password?

    _____

6. What is the vty password?

    _____

7. Turn the router off, if it is on. The router's startup configuration file should already be erased. Doing so makes the router prompt you to enter the Initial Configuration Dialog. This is another term for the System Configuration Dialog.

8. Start the attached computer into Windows, if necessary. To open the HyperTerminal connection you created in Lab 6.2, click **Start**, point to **Programs**, point to **Accessories**, point to **Communications**, and then click **HyperTerminal**. Double-click the **Cisco** connection icon.

9. Turn on the router attached to your PC. If necessary, press **Enter** to get screen output. In a few seconds, you should see router activity display.

10. You may see a message that the NVRAM is invalid, possibly due to write erase. That is because your instructor has erased the startup configuration file or because the router is new and has never had a startup configuration.

11. Next, you are asked if you want to enter the initial configuration dialog. Press **y** for yes and press **Enter**. Notice that using the Ctrl+C key combination on the keyboard takes you out of the Initial Configuration Dialog. This is sometimes necessary as there is no way to go back and reenter an incorrect entry.

12. Next you are asked if you want to enter basic management setup. The basic management setup configures only enough connectivity to manage the router. The router will not be fully functional. You should press **n** for no and then press **Enter**. This puts you into extended setup.

13. When asked if you would like to see the current interface summary, press **Enter** to accept the default answer shown in square brackets, which, in this case, is yes. The summary shows which interfaces are physically on the router. Remember that you will not necessarily configure all the displayed interfaces. Your configuration depends on the router you are configuring and on the information in Figure 6-2.

14. Continue to configure your router, using the responses shown in Table 6-1 as your guide. The responses in the table are for the lab-c router. Tailor them to your router as shown in Figure 6-2 and the information you recorded in Steps 1 through 6 of this lab. As you move through the configuration process, note that valuable information is presented to you on the screen. Be sure to read everything that comes up. Eventually, your configuration is displayed and you are prompted to end the System Configuration Dialog by choosing option 0, 1, or 2. Choose **2** and press **Enter**. This saves your configuration to NVRAM and exits the System Configuration Dialog.

Table 6-1   Configuration responses

When You See This	Type or Press
Enter host name [Router]:	lab-c
Enter enable secret:	class
Enter enable password:	cisco
Enter virtual terminal password:	cisco
Configure SNMP Network Management? [yes]:	n
Configure bridging? [no]:	Enter
Configure DECnet? [no]:	Enter
Configure AppleTalk? [no]:	Enter
Configure IPX? [no]:	Enter
Configure IP? [yes]:	Enter
Configure IGRP routing? [yes]:	n
Configure RIP routing? [no]:	y
Do you want to configure Ethernet0 interface? [yes]:	Enter

Table 6-1   Configuration responses (continued)

When You See This	Type or Press
Configure IP on this interface? [yes]:	Enter
IP address for this interface:	223.8.151.1
Subnet Mask for this interface [255.255.255.0]:	Enter
Do you want to configure Serial0 interface? [yes]:	Enter
Configure IP on this interface? [yes]:	Enter
Configure IP unnumbered on this interface? [no]:	Enter
IP address for this interface:	204.204.7.1
Subnet Mask for this interface [255.255.255.0]:	Enter
Do you want to configure Serial1 interface? [yes]:	Enter
Configure IP on this interface? [yes]:	Enter
Configure IP unnumbered on this interface? [no]:	Enter
IP address for this interface:	199.6.13.2
Subnet Mask for this interface [255.255.255.0]:	Enter

15. There is an additional way to access the Initial Configuration Dialog other than being prompted for it automatically as a consequence of having erased the contents of NVRAM. You can use the setup command at the privileged EXEC mode prompt. Press **Enter** if necessary to reach the user EXEC mode prompt. What does this prompt look like?

_____

16. Type **enable** and press **Enter** to access privileged EXEC mode, which is also known as enable mode. You should be prompted for the enable secret password you configured in the System Configuration Dialog. How do you know you are being prompted for the enable secret password and not the enable password?

_____

_____

17. Type **class** and press **Enter**. How did the prompt change?

_____

18. Enter the **setup** command to access the Initial Configuration Dialog. When prompted to enter the Initial Configuration Dialog, press **y** for yes and press **Enter**.

19. Press **Ctrl+C** to abort the configuration and exit the system configuration dialog.

20. Type **logout**, press **Enter**, close HyperTerminal, and then turn off the router.

Certification Objectives

Objectives for the CCNA exam:

➤ Prepare the initial configuration of your router and enable IP

➤ Check an initial configuration using the setup command

Review Questions

1. When configuring a router, when would you choose basic management setup rather than extended setup?

2. Which passwords are you prompted for when using the Initial Configuration Dialog?

3. What does the current interface summary show you?

4. How can you break out of setup if you make a mistake?

5. What do square brackets [ ] in a prompt for input indicate?

6. Under what condition are you automatically prompted to enter the Initial Configuration Dialog?

7. What command and prompt puts you into the Initial Configuration Dialog?

8. Why is it important to configure an enable or enable secret password on a router?

LAB 6.4 CONFIGURE CONSOLE AND AUX PASSWORDS

Objectives

In Lab 6.3 you were prompted for the vty (virtual terminal) password in addition to the enable and enable secret passwords when configuring the router using the System

Configuration Dialog. The vty password restricts access to the router via Telnet. The vty password is an example of a line password because you are getting a line into the router.

Besides vty, there are two additional lines into the router. You can access the router through the console line and use a console password, which restricts access to the router through the console port. You can also access it through the auxiliary line by using the aux password, which restricts access through the aux port via a modem. Note that neither password is configured when using the System Configuration Dialog. Note also that a console password is not currently required when accessing your router via the console port.

In this lab, you will configure the console and aux passwords for the internetworking lab shown in Figure 6-2.

After completing this lab you will be able to:

➤ Configure the console and aux passwords on a router

Materials Required

This lab requires the following:

➤ The internetworking lab setup in Lab 6.3

➤ HyperTerminal configured to access the routers via the console port, per Lab 6.2

Estimated completion time: **45 minutes**

ACTIVITY

1. If necessary, start the computer into Windows and begin the HyperTerminal session with the router.

2. Turn on the router if necessary. Press **Enter** to get the user EXEC mode prompt, which should be the name of the router (for example, lab-e) and the greater than sign (>).

3. Type **ena** and press **Enter** to access privileged EXEC mode. Why didn't you have to type out the entire command?

_____

4. Type **class** and press **Enter** when prompted for the password. The prompt should change. For example, if the router name is lab-e, the prompt should change to lab-e#.

5. Type **configure terminal** and press **Enter** to enter global configuration mode. What did the prompt change to?

_____

6. Type **line console 0** and press **Enter**. This tells the router that you want to configure the console port. The prompt should change to indicate that you are in line configuration mode. What did the prompt change to?

_____

7. Type **login** to require users to log in when accessing this port and press **Enter**.

8. Type **password cisco** and press **Enter**.

9. Type **exit** and press **Enter**. How many levels does the exit command take you back?

_____

10. Type **line aux 0** and press **Enter**. This tells the router that you want to configure the aux port.

11. Type **login** to require users to log in when accessing this port and press **Enter**.

12. Type **password cisco** and press **Enter**.

13. Press **Ctrl+Z**. To what prompt does this key combination take you back?

_____

14. Press **Enter** after you receive the message that the router has been configured by the console.

15. Type **show run** and press **Enter** to see the running configuration. Notice that the enable secret password is encrypted and looks nothing like "class," which is the password you entered during the System Configuration Dialog.

16. Press the **spacebar** to see more of the display.

17. Notice the console, aux, and vty password information. Are these passwords encrypted?

_____

18. Type **copy run start** and press **Enter**. Press **Enter** again to accept startup-config as the destination filename. What does the copy run start command do?

_____

19. Is it really necessary to use this copy run start command, or are the configuration changes automatically saved?

_____

20. Type **logout** and press **Enter** to exit the router.

Certification Objectives

Objectives for the CCNA exam:

➤ Manage configuration files from the privileged EXEC mode

➤ Control router passwords, identification, and banner

➤ Log in to a router in both user and privileged modes

Review Questions

1. Which passwords are you not prompted for when using the System Configuration Dialog?

2. Which mode must you be in to configure the vty, console, and auxiliary passwords?

3. What does the prompt look like if you are in the mode that is the correct answer for Review Question #2?

4. What two commands are used to create the line passwords after you are at the prompt you specified in Review Question 3?

5. What is the only router password encrypted by default?

LAB 6.5 USE HELP, THE COMMAND HISTORY, ENHANCED EDITING FEATURES, AND THE SHOW COMMAND

Objectives

The objective of this lab is to give you experience in accessing command-line help, using the Cisco enhanced editing features and command history, and using the very important show commands to determine information about your router.

With a little experience, you can figure out how to do almost anything on a Cisco router or switch using command-line help. In addition, the enhanced editing features of the command exec allow you to move around commands quickly and avoid retyping previously used commands. You use show commands to monitor and verify what you have configured in the router. In this lab, you will use command-line help and various show commands, and you will edit the command line using the editing features of the Cisco command executive.

After completing this lab you will be able to:

➤ Get help with commands

➤ Navigate the command line more efficiently

➤ Understand the kinds of information you can obtain using the most popular show commands

Materials Required

This lab requires the following:

➤ Completion of Labs 6.1, 6.3, and 6.4

➤ HyperTerminal configured to access the routers via the console port, per Lab 6.2

6

Estimated completion time: **60 minutes**

ACTIVITY

1. Start the computer into Windows if necessary, and begin the HyperTerminal session with the router.

2. Turn on the router if necessary. Press **Enter**. Which password are you being prompted for?

   _____

3. Enter the password you configured in Lab 6.4.

   _____

4. After the correct password is entered, your cursor should be at the user EXEC mode prompt, which should be the name of the router and the greater than sign (for example, lab-e>). Verify that this has occurred.

5. Type **?**. There is no need to press **Enter**. A list of commands should be displayed. Press the **spacebar** to scroll through the list. What do these commands represent?

   _____

6. Type **show ?**. A list of commands should appear. What do these commands represent?

   _____

Notice that the show start and show run commands cannot be used in user EXEC mode.

7. Complete the show command by typing **hosts** and pressing **Enter**. Does your router know the names of any other routers? Why or why not?

   _____

   _____

8. Type **show version** and press **Enter**. What is the name of the IOS image file?

   _____

   _____

9. What version of the IOS is your router running?

   _____

10. Press the **spacebar** to scroll through the display.

11. Type **ena** and press Enter to access enable mode.

12. Type **class** and press **Enter** when prompted for the enable secret password. How did the prompt change?

    _____

13. Type **?**. Press the **spacebar** to scroll through the commands. What do these commands represent?

    _____

14. Type **show ?**. What do these commands represent? Why are there so many more commands in enable mode than in user mode?

    _____

    _____

15. Use the **show flash** command to display information about the flash. What is the IOS filename? Your answer should be the same as what was recorded in Step 8.

    _____

    _____

    How big is the file?

    _____

16. Type **show protocol** and press **Enter**. What protocol is enabled on your router?

    _____

17. What interface and address information appears?

    _____

18. Type **show arp** and press **Enter**. What information does this command display?

    _____

19. Type **clear ?** and look for the command to clear the contents of the arp table. What do you think the command is?

    _____

20. Backspace over the word "clear" to erase it. Type **show start** and press **Enter**. What are you viewing the contents of?

    _____

21. What is the hostname of the router?

_____

22. What interfaces are available for configuration on the router?

_____

23. What interfaces are actually configured on the router?

_____

24. Is a routing protocol configured on the router? If so, what is it?

_____

25. Type **show run** and press **Enter**. What are you viewing the contents of?

_____

26. Is the running configuration supposed to be the same as the startup configuration? Explain your answer.

_____

_____

_____

_____

27. Type **show history** and press **Enter**. What appears?

_____

28. Press the **up arrow** until you see the show start command. What does the up arrow do?

_____

29. Press the **down arrow** until you see the show history command. What does the down arrow do?

_____

30. Press **Ctrl+A**. What does this do?

_____

31. Press **Ctrl+E**. What does this do?

_____

32. Press **Esc+B**. What does this do?

_____

33. Press **Esc+F**. What does this do?

_____

34. Delete the command by pressing the **backspace** key. Type **terminal his** and press the **Tab** key. What does this do?

_____

_____

35. Use context-sensitive help to determine for what the terminal history size command is used.

_____

36. Change the history buffer size to 20 using the **terminal history size 20** command.

37. Enter the **show history** command again. You changed the buffer from the default of 10 to 20. Are there more than 10 entries in the buffer? Do you expect that an increased buffer size would require more router memory use?

_____

38. Type **logout** and press **Enter** to exit the router. Close HyperTerminal and turn off the router.

Certification Objectives

Objectives for the CCNA exam:

➤ Log in to a router in both user and privileged modes

➤ Use the context-sensitive help facility

➤ Use the command history and editing features

➤ Identify the main Cisco IOS software commands for router startup

➤ Examine router elements

Review Questions

1. Within the lab exercise, what exactly did the "?" show you?

2. Is the "?" prompt sensitive?

3. Which two commands display information about the IOS file?

4. What command increases the history size?

5. What is the key combination that has the same result as pressing the up arrow?

CHAPTER SEVEN

ROUTER STARTUP AND CONFIGURATION

Labs included in this chapter

➤ Lab 7.1 Configure IP Addresses and IP Hosts
➤ Lab 7.2 Install, Configure, and Use a TFTP Server
➤ Lab 7.3 Configure a Message and Interface Description
➤ Lab 7.4 Using the CDP, Ping, Trace, and Telnet Commands
➤ Lab 7.5 Copy and Paste Router Configurations
➤ Lab 7.6 Using Boot System Commands and the Configuration Register

CCNA Exam Objectives	
Objective	Lab
Configure IP addresses	7.1
Verify IP addresses	7.1
Prepare to backup, upgrade, and load a backup Cisco IOS software image	7.2
List the commands to load Cisco IOS software from flash memory, a TFTP server, or ROM	7.6
Control router passwords, identification, and banner	7.3
Log in to a router in both user and privileged modes	7.1, 7.2, 7.3, 7.4, 7.5, 7.6
Use the command history and editing features	7.4
Identify the functions performed by ICMP	7.4
Identify the main Cisco IOS software commands for router startup	7.6

LAB 7.1 CONFIGURE IP ADDRESSES AND IP HOSTS

Objectives

The objective of this lab is to give you experience in configuring IP addresses without the aid of the System Configuration Dialog. In addition, you will make IP to hostname mappings. IP to host name mappings can be configured using a name server or in this case, the router. In this lab, you will use the IP address command to configure the router interfaces, and the IP host command to provide IP to host name mappings.

After completing this lab you will be able to:

➤ Configure IP addresses for each interface on the router

➤ Configure IP to host name mappings using the IP host command

Materials Required

This lab requires the following:

➤ The internetworking lab setup shown in Figure 7-1

➤ Completion of all labs in Chapter 6

Estimated completion time: **45 minutes**

ACTIVITY

1. Start the computer into Windows, and begin the HyperTerminal session with the router.

2. Turn on the router and hubs if necessary. Press **Enter** to start, and type the console line password **cisco** to get to the user EXEC mode prompt.

3. Type **ena** and press **Enter** to access privileged EXEC mode.

4. Type **class** and press **Enter** when prompted for the enable secret password.

5. Type **conf t** and press **Enter**. What is the name of this mode?

_____

6. Enter a name table into the router. Put all routers in the name table, including the one you are configuring. Refer to Figure 7-1 for router hostname and IP addressing information. Type **ip host**, the name of the first router in the lab, which is lab-a, and all IP addresses associated with the interfaces on this first router. Remote routers will attempt to access the named router via the IP addresses in order of how you list them. Press **Enter**. The first lab router is the lab-a router, so you should have typed the following:
ip hostlab-a 192.5.5.1 205.7.5.1 201.100.11.1

Note that the addresses in this example are the interfaces listed in the network diagram in Figure 7-1.

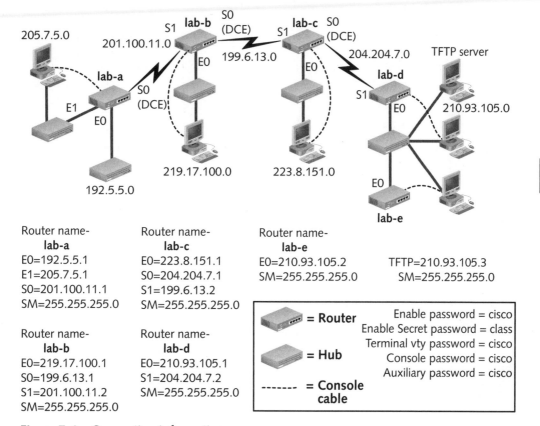

Figure 7-1   Connection information

7. Repeat Step 6 for all routers. Each router should eventually have the IP addresses of all router interfaces in the internetwork.

8. Press **Ctrl+Z** to exit global configuration mode. Press **Enter** to clear the message.

9. What is the value of the IP host command?

_____

10. Type **show host** and press **Enter**. What hosts does your router know about?

_____

11. Next, you will configure the active router interfaces for IP addresses. Type **conf t** and press **Enter**.

12. Type **int e0** (int e0/0 for 2600 series routers) and press **Enter**. What mode are you in, and what will the next commands you type affect?

_____

13. To configure the IP address of the Ethernet 0 interface, type the following:

    ip address [*IP address of your router's e0 interface*] [*subnet mask*]

    No shutdown

    Use Figure 7-1 to determine the IP address of your router's E0 interface.

14. What does the first command line in the example in Step 13 do?

    _____

15. What does the second line do?

    _____

16. Using Steps 12 and 13 as an example, configure the IP addresses of any additional interfaces that are to be configured on your router, per Figure 7-1. If you are configuring an S0 interface, you will need three commands instead of two. S0 has arbitrarily been chosen to perform the clocking function for the WAN links. Typically, the Telco's CSU/DSU or other device does the clocking (DCE) outside of the lab environment. Make sure to add the following configuration command for S0 if you have an active S0 interface:

    Clockrate 56000

17. When finished configuring all interfaces on your router, as shown in Figure 7-1, press **Ctrl+Z** to return to the enable prompt.

18. Type **show run** to view the running configuration. There will be additional information in the running configuration that you did not configure. This consists of default router settings that are automatically configured and beyond the scope of the CCNA exam. Figure 7-2 displays the correct running configuration for the lab-c router.

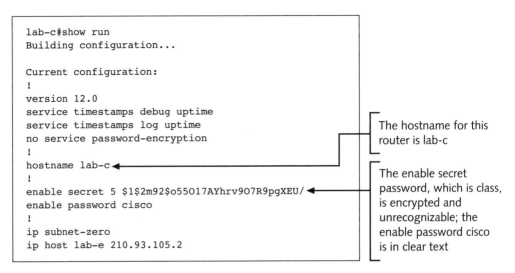

```
lab-c#show run
Building configuration...

Current configuration:
!
version 12.0
service timestamps debug uptime
service timestamps log uptime
no service password-encryption
!
hostname lab-c
!
enable secret 5 $1$2m92$o55017AYhrv9O7R9pgXEU/
enable password cisco
!
ip subnet-zero
ip host lab-e 210.93.105.2
```

The hostname for this router is lab-c

The enable secret password, which is class, is encrypted and unrecognizable; the enable password cisco is in clear text

Figure 7-2   Output of the show run command

```
ip host lab-d 210.93.105.1 204.204.7.2
ip host lab-c 223.8.151.1 204.204.7.1 199.6.13.2
ip host lab-b 219.17.100.1 199.6.13.1 201.100.11.2
ip host lab-a 192.5.5.1 205.7.5.1 201.100.11.1
!
!
!
!
interface Ethernet0
 ip address 223.8.151.1 255.255.255.0
 no ip directed-broadcast
 no mop enabled
!
interface Serial0
 ip address 204.204.7.1 255.255.255.0
 no ip directed-broadcast
 no ip mroute-cache
 no fair-queue
 clockrate 56000
!
interface Serial1
 ip address 199.6.13.2 255.255.255.0
 no ip directed-broadcast
!
router rip
 redistribute connected
 network 199.6.13.0
 network 204.204.7.0
 network 223.8.151.0
!
no ip http server
ip classless
!
dialer-list 1 protocol ip permit
dialer-list 1 protocol ipx permit
!
line con 0
 password cisco
 login
 transport input none
line aux 0
 password cisco
 login
line vty 0 4
 password cisco
 login
!
end
```

The host name table allows you to use names rather than IP addresses when referring to the routers

Notice the clockrate command configured on the S0 interface

RIP is configured using major network numbers of connected networks

Console, auxiliary, and vty passwords are configured with the password cisco

Figure 7-2   Output of the show run command (continued)

19. Check all commands and IP addresses, router RIP network numbers, and IP host addresses. RIP was configured automatically via the System Configuration Dialog in Lab 6-3. The network numbers listed for RIP should be the networks directly connected to your router. If there are no mistakes, proceed to Step 24.

20. If there is a mistake in the interface configurations, return to Steps 11 through 18 and reconfigure the interfaces. Then go to Step 24.

21. If there is a mistake in the router RIP, type **conf t** and press **Enter** to enter global configuration mode. Then type **no router rip** and press **Enter** to remove the incorrect RIP information. Now type **router rip** to enter router configuration mode. Enter the correct numbers of the networks that are directly attached to your router, using this command as an example:

    network 210.93.105.0

22. Continue to use the network command until all networks attached to your router are listed. For example, the lab-a router will have three network command lines, because it is attached to three networks. Remember to use major network numbers, not interface addresses. When finished, press **Ctrl+Z** to return to enable mode.

23. If there is no mistake in the list of IP hostnames, go to Step 24. If there is a mistake in the list of IP hostnames, type **conf t** and press **Enter**. Then type **no ip host** followed by the name of the router that has the error. Go to Steps 6 through 8, and reconfigure the IP to hostname mappings. When you are sure it is correct, proceed to Step 24.

24. Type **copy run start** at the enable prompt, and press **Enter** to replace the startup configuration file. Press **Enter** again to accept the default destination filename.

25. Type **logout** to exit the router.

Certification Objectives

Objectives for the CCNA exam:

➤ Configure IP addresses.

➤ Verify IP addresses.

➤ Log in to a router in both user and privileged modes.

Review Questions

1. What mode must you be in to configure IP addresses on a Cisco router?

2. What is the purpose of a hostname table?

3. What is the command to point to another router or server for hostname resolution?

4. What is the clockrate command used for?

5. What does the no shutdown command do?

LAB 7.2 INSTALL, CONFIGURE, AND USE A TFTP SERVER

Objectives

The objective of this lab is to show you the benefit of having a TFTP server on your network to configure the routers in the event they lose their IOS or configuration information. If you completed the labs in Chapter 6 and Lab 7.1 properly, your routers are configured to match the internetworking lab setup shown in Figure 7-1. It is now appropriate to copy these configurations to a TFTP server.

There is more than one kind of TFTP software. One of the easiest to use is Cisco's own TFTPServ.exe. In this lab, you will add a computer to the internetworking lab on the hub between routers lab-d and lab-e. This corresponds to network 210.93.105.0, as shown in Figure 7-1. You will then install and configure the TFTP server software. Last, you will copy the IOS and the router configuration files to the TFTP server.

After completing this lab you will be able to:

➤ Install and configure TFTP server software

➤ Copy the Cisco IOS from the router to the TFTP server

➤ Copy router configurations to the TFTP server

Materials Required

This lab requires the following:

➤ Completion of all labs in Chapter 6

➤ Completion of Lab 7.1

➤ A Windows computer with a NIC configured and the TCP/IP protocol configured

➤ UTP patch cable

➤ TFTP server software on a floppy disk

Estimated completion time: **45 minutes**

ACTIVITY

1. Place the TFTP server in close proximity to the computer attached to the lab-e router, as shown in Figure 7-1.

2. Attach one end of the UTP patch cable to the NIC on the TFTP server.

3. Attach the other end of the UTP patch cable to the hub between router lab-d and router lab-e, as shown in Figure 7-1.

4. Turn on the computer and let it start into Windows.

5. Put the floppy disk with the TFTP server software on it in drive A of the TFTP server.

6. Click **Start** and then click **Run**.

7. Click the **Browse** button to search for an executable file on drive A. Double-click the executable file and then click **OK** to install the TFTP server software. Accept any defaults presented during the installation.

8. Right-click **Network Neighborhood** and click **Properties**.

9. Click the **Configuration** tab if necessary.

10. Double-click **TCP/IP**.

11. If the server patch cable has been attached to the hub between router lab-d and router lab-e, the network is 210.93.105.0, as shown in Figure 7-1. This figure shows that the E0 interfaces on routers lab-d and lab-e are using 210.93.105.1 and 210.93.105.2, respectively. Using this example, the next available host number for the TFTP server is 210.93.105.3. Assign the IP address **210.93.105.3** to the TFTP server.

12. You also need to provide the subnet mask for the TFTP server. It should be the same as the network to which it is attached, which, in this example, is **255.255.255.0**.

13. A gateway must be configured on the network hosts so that they can get out to the rest of the internetwork or to the Internet. Typically, the gateway is the Ethernet interface on the router that is closest to the host that is being configured. In this example, the gateway is 210.93.105.1, which is the Ethernet interface on the lab-d router, as shown in Figure 7-1. Configure the correct gateway for the IFTP server.

14. Click **OK** twice. You will be prompted to restart the computer. Make sure there is no floppy disk in Drive A. Click **Yes** to restart.

15. After the computer restarts, open the TFTP program by clicking **Start**, pointing to **Programs**, and then clicking the name of the TFTP program; you can also double-click a desktop shortcut if one exists.

16. Move to a router terminal, and start the computer into Windows if necessary.

17. Begin the HyperTerminal session with a router.

18. Turn on the router and hubs if necessary. Press **Enter** to start, and then type **cisco** for the user EXEC mode password.

19. Type **ena** and press **Enter** to access privileged EXEC mode.

20. Type **class** and press **Enter** when prompted for the enable secret password.

21. What command will you type to look at the active configuration?

_____

Use the command you recorded in the Step 21, and double check to make sure it has been configured correctly, per Figure 7-1.

22. Ping the TFTP server to make sure you have connectivity to it. Type **ping** followed by **210.93.105.3**, which is the IP address you configured on the TFTP server. Press **Enter**. If your ping fails, use the **show interface** command to make sure all of your configured interfaces are up/up. Perhaps your team members are having problems that may be affecting your ping. Also, make sure you check all physical connections and the TCP/IP configuration on the TFTP server. When you can ping the TFTP server successfully, proceed to the next step.

23. Type **copy run tftp** and press **Enter** to begin the process of backing up the running configuration to the TFTP server. This command will eventually fail if the TFTP server software is not running.

24. Next you are prompted for the IP address of the TFTP server. Type **210.93.105.3** and press **Enter**.

25. You are prompted for the name of the configuration file. Type the hostname of your router followed by **–config**. For example, the lab-e configuration file should be named lab-e-config. Press **Enter**. Look at the screen on the TFTP server for an indication of success.

26. Type **show flash** and press **Enter**. What is the name of the IOS image of the router? Look at the name carefully. Depending on the font style being used in HyperTerminal, it can be very difficult to tell the difference between a lower case L and the number one.

_____

27. Backing up the configuration files is typically very fast as these files are small. Conversely, the IOS file is relatively large and takes much more time to back up. Because the same IOS file is probably running on all the routers in the lab, only the person configuring the lab-e router should back up the IOS, which begins on Step 28. The other team members should observe the process.

28. Type **copy flash tftp** to begin the process of backing up the router operating system (IOS) on the TFTP server.

29. You are prompted for the source filename. Type the name of the file you recorded in Step 26 and press **Enter**.

7

30. Next, you are prompted for the IP address of the TFTP server. Type **210.93.105.3**, and press **Enter**.

31. Finally, you are prompted for the destination filename. The default (indicated in square brackets) is the same name you typed for the source filename in Step 29. Press **Enter** to accept the default.

32. A series of exclamation marks on your screen indicates the IOS is copying to the TFTP server. The backup process can take 5 to 15 minutes.

33. When the process is finished, go to the TFTP server, and search for the backed-up files on the hard drive. When the router lab is completely backed up, you should have five configuration files and one IOS file on the TFTP server.

34. Log out of the router.

Certification Objectives

Objectives for the CCNA exam:

➤ Prepare to back up, upgrade, and load a back up Cisco IOS software image

➤ Log in to a router in both user and privileged modes

Review Questions

1. What is the purpose of a TFTP server?

2. What is the purpose of a default gateway?

3. What prompt and command are used to copy the active configuration to a TFTP server?

4. What prompt and command are used to copy the IOS to a TFTP server?

5. List two show commands that display the IOS image filename.

LAB 7.3 CONFIGURE A MESSAGE AND INTERFACE DESCRIPTION

Objectives

The objective of this lab is to show you how to customize your router further by configuring a message of the day and by assigning descriptions to interfaces. In this lab, you will use the banner motd command and the description command to customize your router.

After completing this lab you will be able to:

➤ Use the banner motd command to provide a message for anyone accessing the router

➤ Use the description command to add a description to a configured interface

Materials Required

This lab requires the following:

➤ Completion of all labs in Chapter 6, as well as Lab 7.1

Estimated completion time: **20 minutes**

ACTIVITY

1. Start the computer into Windows, and begin a HyperTerminal session with the router.

2. Turn on the router and hubs if necessary. Press **Enter** to start and type the password **cisco** to get to the user EXEC mode prompt.

3. Type **ena** and press **Enter** to access privileged EXEC mode.

4. Type **class** and press **Enter** when prompted for the enable secret password.

5. Type **conf t** and press **Enter** to enter global configuration mode.

6. Type **banner motd #** and press **Enter**. What message appears?

_____

7. Type **Welcome to the Cisco 2500 series router**.

8. Type **#** and press **Enter** to signal the end of your message. Press **Ctrl+Z** to exit global configuration mode.

9. Type **exit** and press **Enter** to logout of the router.

10. When prompted by the router, press **Enter** to start. You should see the message of the day.

11. Enter the password **cisco** to get to the user EXEC mode prompt.

12. Type **ena** and press **Enter** to access enable mode.

13. Type **class** and press **Enter** when prompted for the enable secret password.

14. Type **conf t** and press **Enter** to enter global configuration mode.

15. Type **no banner motd** and press **Enter**. This removes the message of the day.

16. From the global configuration mode prompt, type **int e0** and press **Enter** to enter interface configuration mode.

17. Type **description Attached to Ethernet LAN lab-e** (substitute the name of your router if necessary) and press **Enter**.

18. Press **Ctrl+Z** to return to the enable prompt.

19. Type **show int e0**. Does the description configured for e0 appear?

_____

20. Copy the running configuration to the startup configuration.

21. Type **logout** to exit the router.

Certification Objectives

Objectives for the CCNA exam:

➤ Control router passwords, identification, and banner.

➤ Log in to a router in both user and privileged modes.

Review Questions

1. What is the purpose of the banner command?

2. What does MOTD stand for?

3. What is the purpose of the description command?

4. What mode must you be in to configure a banner?

5. What mode must you be in to configure a description?

LAB 7.4 USING THE CDP, PING, TRACE, AND TELNET COMMANDS

Objectives

The Cisco Discovery Protocol (CDP) shares configuration information between locally connected Cisco devices. The various show CDP commands tell you about routers and switches that are directly connected to your router. The ping and trace commands provide connectivity information at the Network layer of the OSI reference model and are used primarily for troubleshooting. Extended mode ping is a more sophisticated type of ping that you will also investigate. The Telnet application provides Application layer connectivity information and lets you access remote routers.

The objective of this lab is to familiarize you with the displayed output of the various show cdp commands as well as other configured CDP commands. In addition, you will become familiar with the troubleshooting commands: ping, extended mode ping, trace, and telnet.

After completing this lab you will:

> ➤ Be familiar with the output generated by the various CDP commands

> ➤ Understand how to test for Network layer connectivity using the ping and trace commands

> ➤ Understand the difference between ping and extended mode ping

> ➤ Know how to use the Telnet application to remotely access routers

Materials Required

This lab requires the following:

> ➤ Completion of all labs in Chapter 6, as well as Lab 7.1

Estimated completion time: **30 minutes**

ACTIVITY

1. Start the computer into Windows, and begin the HyperTerminal session with the router.

2. Turn on the router and hubs if necessary. Press **Enter** to start, and type the password **cisco** to get to the user EXEC mode prompt.

3. Type **ena** and press **Enter** to access enable mode.

4. Type **class** and press **Enter** when prompted for the enable secret password.

5. Type **show cdp neighbor** and press **Enter** to get information regarding your directly connected neighbors. If you are unable to see your neighbors, use the

show interface command and make sure the status of each of your interfaces is up/up. What is one of your neighbors?

_____

What local interface is the neighbor on?

_____

What kind of device is it (capability)?

_____

What other information does this show command provide?

_____

_____

_____

6. Press the **up arrow** until you get to the show cdp neighbor command. Press the **spacebar** once, and then type **detail**, and press **Enter**. What additional information do you get when you add "detail" to the show CDP neighbor command?

_____

_____

7. Type **show cdp interface** and press **Enter**. What is the default broadcast interval for CDP?

_____

8. Type **conf t** and press **Enter** to enter global configuration mode.

9. Type **cdp timer 90** and press **Enter**. Exit to enable mode, and enter the **show cdp interface** command once again. Were you successful in changing the broadcast interval to 90 seconds?

_____

_____

10. Enter global configuration mode. Type **int e0** and press **Enter**.

11. Type **no cdp enable** and press **Enter**. What does this command do?

_____

12. Press **Ctrl+Z** to return to enable mode, and enter the **show CDP interface** command. Has CDP been disabled on E0?

_____

How do you know?

_____

13. Reenable CDP on the interface using the **cdp enable** command in interface configuration mode.

14. Enter **Ctrl+Z** to return to enable mode. Can you confirm that CDP has been reenabled on the E0 interface?

_____

15. Type **ping** and then type an IP address of a remote router interface. For example, if you are on the lab-b router and want to check for connectivity to the lab-d, S1 interface, you would type **ping 204.204.7.2** and press **Enter**.

16. Was the ping successful?

_____

If not, attempt to ping several other interfaces. What symbol indicates a successful ping?

_____

If your ping succeeded, what were the minimum, average, and maximum roundtrip times?

_____

17. Type **ping** and press **Enter**. How does the extended mode ping command respond?

_____

18. Press **Enter** to accept the default protocol. Enter any remote IP address. Change the repeat count to 20. Change the datagram size to 1500. Continue to press **Enter** to accept the defaults for the remaining prompts. How does this output differ from the output from the ping command you issued in Step 15?

_____

_____

19. Type **trace** and then type the IP address of an interface on the farthest remote router from your location. For example, if you are on the lab-b router and want to check for connectivity to the E0 interface on the lab-e router type, **trace 210.93.105.2** and press **Enter**.

 If locked into an unsuccessful trace, break out by pressing **Ctrl+Shift+6**.

20. Was the trace successful?

_____

What information is obtained from the trace command?

_____

What is the advantage of using the trace command instead of the ping command?

_____

7

21. At which layer of the OSI reference model do ping and trace operate?

_____

22. At which layer of the TCP/IP reference model do ping and trace operate?

_____

23. What underlying protocol controls the messages from ping and trace as well as manages the work of IP in general?

_____

24. Type **telnet** and then type the IP address of an interface on a remote router. For example, if you are on the lab-b router and want to telnet to the lab-e router, type **telnet 210.93.105.2** and press **Enter**.

    Alternatively, you could just use the name of the router to which you would like to connect. For example, you could type **lab-e** and press **Enter**.

    What makes it possible to use names instead of IP addresses when telnetting? (_Hint_: See Lab 7.1.)

    _____

    Did the telnet succeed?

    _____

25. If the telnet failed, try telnetting to a different router until you can telnet successfully. Ask your instructor for help if necessary.

26. You should be prompted for a password when you telnet successfully. Type **cisco** and press **Enter**. Is this the same kind of password you are prompted for when you log on to a router locally?

    _____

    Exactly what kind of password is this?

    _____

27. Type **ena** and press **Enter** to access enable mode.

28. Type **class** and press **Enter** when prompted for the enable secret password.

29. Type **show run** and press **Enter**. Exactly what is displayed?

    _____

30. Type **show cdp neigh det** and press **Enter**. What is the advantage of using the telnet application in conjunction with the show cdp neighbor command?

    _____

31. At which layer of the OSI reference model is telnet operating?

    _____

32. At which layer of the TCP/IP reference model is telnet operating?

    _____

33. As a troubleshooting tool, what advantages does telnet have over ping and trace?

34. Type **logout** and press **Enter** to terminate your telnet session.

35. Type **logout** and press **Enter** to exit your router.

Certification Objectives

Objectives for the CCNA exam:

➤ Use the command history and editing features

➤ Identify the functions performed by ICMP

➤ Log in to a router in both user and privileged modes

Review Questions

1. What is the purpose of the CDP protocol?

2. Is CDP enabled by default on all Cisco routers?

3. What is the difference between ping and extended mode ping?

4. What mode and command are used to disable CDP on an interface?

5. What mode and command are used to disable CDP on the entire router?

LAB 7.5 COPY AND PASTE ROUTER CONFIGURATIONS

Objectives

In Lab 6.2, you practiced backing up the IOS and configuration files to a TFTP server. Configuration files are small and can easily be stored on a floppy disk or a computer hard drive as a simple text file. If you have local access to the router, it is faster to use the following method to save configuration files than using a TFTP server. The objective of this lab is to demonstrate how to save and retrieve your router configuration files locally.

In this lab, you will copy the running configuration of the router to a text file, using Notepad. Next, you will erase the startup configuration of the router and then reload and paste the saved router configuration back into the router.

After completing this lab you will be able to:

> Save the router configuration locally using the Notepad application

> Erase the startup configuration of the router

> Re-create the running and startup configurations of the router by pasting the saved text file into the running configuration of the router

Materials Required

This lab requires the following:

> Completion of all labs in Chapter 6, as well as Lab 7.1

> The Notepad application

Estimated completion time: **30 minutes**

ACTIVITY

1. If necessary, turn on the workstations.

2. Create a folder on the desktop. Name it with your own last name.

3. Open the HyperTerminal program and create a session with the router.

4. If necessary, turn on the routers and hubs.

5. Press **Enter** to get started, and type the console password **cisco** to get to the user EXEC mode prompt.

6. Enter enable mode using **class** as the enable secret password.

7. Display the running configuration. Which command did you use?

_____

8. Press the **spacebar** until the entire configuration has been displayed.

9. Scroll up until you see the words "hostname lab-a." Your hostname may differ, depending on the router you are configuring.

10. Use the mouse to highlight from (and including) the words **hostname lab-a** at the beginning of the configuration to (and including) the word **end** at the end of the configuration.

11. Right-click the highlighted text, and click **Copy**.

12. Open the Notepad program by clicking **Start**, pointing to **Programs**, pointing to **Accessories**, and then clicking **Notepad**.

13. Maximize the window.

14. Right-click in the Notepad window, and then click **Paste**.

15. If the word "Paste" is not an option in the pop-up menu, return to the running configuration and attempt to copy it to the Clipboard again. If the words are going off the screen to the right, word wrap is not enabled. In this case, click **Edit**, and then click **Word Wrap** to enable it.

16. When you have successfully pasted the configuration into Notepad, save the file as **lab-a-config** (substitute your router's hostname) in the folder you created on the desktop.

17. **Minimize** the Notepad program and return to HyperTerminal.

18. At the enable prompt, type **erase start**, and then press **Enter**. Confirm the erase.

19. Type **show start** and press **Enter**. What does the erase start command do?

_____

20. Use the **reload** command to restart the router. If prompted to save the configuration, press **N** for no. **Confirm** the reload and let the router restart. The router may take a few minutes to reload. You should eventually get to the Router> prompt or a similar prompt that indicates your prior configuration has been erased.

21. If prompted to enter the initial configuration dialog, press **N** for no, and then press **Enter**.

22. If prompted to terminate autoinstall, press **Enter** to accept the default answer of Yes.

23. Enter privileged EXEC mode.

24. Enter global configuration mode.

25. Restore the Notepad window.

26. Click **Edit**, and then click **Select All** from the Notepad menu.

27. Right-click the selection, and then click **Copy** from the menu.

28. Minimize Notepad, and right-click beside the router prompt.

29. Click **Paste to Host** from the pop-up menu.

30. When the router display stops scrolling, press **Enter** and display the running configuration on the router using the appropriate command. Does it appear to be correct?

_____

If it is not correct, get help from your teammates or instructor.

31. Type **show interface** and press **Enter**. What is the status of each of your interfaces?

_____

_____

_____

32. If any of your interfaces are administratively down, and you are using those interfaces, you should enter interface configuration mode for those interfaces and issue the **no shutdown** command. Interfaces often administratively go down when their configurations are obtained via pasting them in as you just did or when they are obtained from a TFTP server using the copy tftp run command.

33. Copy the running configuration to the startup configuration.

34. Log out of the router.

35. Close the Notepad program.

36. Delete the folder and file from the Windows desktop.

Certification Objectives

Objectives for the CCNA exam:

➤ Log in to a router in both user and privileged modes.

Review Questions

1. Why is it a good idea to save your router configuration files to a hard drive or floppy disk?

2. Where does the startup configuration live and how do you erase it?

3. What do you think would happen if you used the erase flash command? (Note that this is for discussion purposes only. Do *not* use this command.)

4. What should you try if your interfaces administratively go down?

5. How can you erase the running configuration?

LAB 7.6 USING BOOT SYSTEM COMMANDS AND THE CONFIGURATION REGISTER

Objectives

When the router starts up, it goes through a specified procedure as outlined in Chapter 7 of your text. The IOS can be loaded from flash memory, ROM, or a TFTP server. By default, the configuration register is set to look to the startup configuration in NVRAM for boot instruction commands. If there are none, the IOS is loaded from flash by default. You can also affect the boot procedure by changing the configuration register.

The objective of this lab is to learn how to examine the configuration register and enter boot system commands into the router's configuration to force the router to boot from a TFTP server or to ROM. You will also learn how to change the configuration register and force the router to boot the IOS from ROM.

After completing this lab you will:

➤ Be familiar with the configuration register and its various settings

➤ Understand the various boot system commands and how to force the router to boot the IOS from a TFTP server or from ROM

Materials Required

This lab requires the following:

➤ Completion of all labs in Chapter 6, as well as Lab 7.1

Estimated completion time: **45 minutes**

ACTIVITY

1. Start the computer into Windows, and begin the HyperTerminal session with the router.

2. Turn on the router and hubs if necessary. Press **Enter** to start, and type the password **cisco** to get to the user EXEC mode prompt.

3. Type **ena** and press **Enter** to access enable mode.

4. Type **class** and press **Enter** when prompted for the enable secret password.

5. Type **ping 210.93.105.3** to make sure you have connectivity to the TFTP server. If you don't have connectivity, check the status of your interfaces by typing **show interface** to make sure you have physical connectivity. You can also trace to the TFTP server to pinpoint where the problem is.

6. Check to make sure the TFTP server software is running on the TFTP server.

7. Type **show version** and press **Enter**. Scroll to the bottom of the command output. What is the name of the IOS image file?

_____

What is the configuration register setting?

_____

From where does this register setting indicate the IOS will be loaded?

_____

8. Type **conf t** and press **Enter** to enter global configuration mode. Only the person configuring the lab-e router will perform Steps 9 through 19, which configure the lab-e router to boot from the TFTP server using the IOS that was previously copied to the server. The other team members should observe this process.

9. Type **boot system tftp [*filename*]**, where filename is the name of the IOS image file you recorded in Step 7.

10. Exit to enable mode.

11. Type **copy run start** and press **Enter**. Press **Enter** again to confirm.

12. Type **reload** and press **Enter**. Press **Enter** again to confirm.

13. When the router reloads, it will look to NVRAM for boot system commands. What tells it to do this?

_____

14. If your boot system command was correctly configured, your router will load the IOS from the TFTP server. It will take approximately 5 to 15 minutes and you will see a series of exclamation marks while it is loading. If it didn't load correctly, you probably made a mistake when entering the filename. Make sure you recorded the filename correctly. Repeat Steps 8 through 12 if necessary.

15. Eventually you should be prompted to press **Return** to get started. Type the password **cisco** to get to the user EXEC mode prompt.

16. Type **ena** and press **Enter** to access enable mode.

17. Type **class** and press **Enter** when prompted for the enable secret password.

18. Type **conf t** and press **Enter** to enter global configuration mode.

19. Type **no boot system tftp [*filename*]**, where filename is the name of the IOS image file you recorded in Step 7.

20. All team members should configure their own routers, beginning with this step. Type **config-register 0x2100** and press **Enter**. Exit to enable mode.

21. Enter the **copy run start** command and confirm to save it as the default name.

22. Type **reload** and press **Enter**. Confirm if necessary.

23. When the router reloads, it will look to NVRAM for boot system commands. When it sees none, it will look at the configuration register. From where does the current configuration register tell the router to boot the IOS?

_____

24. What does the ROM Monitor mode prompt look like?

_____

_____

25. The commands in ROM Monitor mode are generally not the same as the commands from the command EXEC you have been using thus far in the labs. At this point, you must change the configuration register back to the value you recorded in Step 7 so that the IOS will once again be loaded from flash memory. Type **o/r 0x2102**. If your configuration register setting in Step 7 is not 0x2102, substitute the register setting you recorded. Press **Enter**.

26. Type **initialize** and press **Enter**.

27. At this point, the router should reload and the bootup procedure should appear as it has in previous labs. Enter the appropriate passwords to enter enable mode, then type **show version** and press **Enter**. Has the configuration register been reset to the default?

_____

28. Log out of the router.

Certification Objectives

Objectives for the CCNA exam:

➤ Log in to a router in both user and privilege modes

➤ List the commands to load Cisco IOS software from flash memory, a TFTP server, or ROM

➤ Identify the main Cisco IOS software commands for router startup

Review Questions

1. What are two ways to control the boot procedure for loading the IOS?

2. What would happen during bootup if the configuration register were set to 0x2101?

3. Why might you want to use a series of boot system commands in your configuration?

NONROUTABLE, ROUTED, AND ROUTING PROTOCOLS

Labs included in this chapter

➤ Lab 8.1 Understanding Terms and Concepts Related to Routing

➤ Lab 8.2 Configure Static Routes

➤ Lab 8.3 Configure RIP

➤ Lab 8.4 Configure IGRP

CCNA Exam Objectives	
Objective	Lab
List problems that each routing type encounters when dealing with topology changes, and describe techniques to reduce the number of these problems	8.1
Add the RIP routing protocol to your configuration	8.3
Add the IGRP routing protocol to your configuration	8.4

LAB 8.1 UNDERSTANDING TERMS AND CONCEPTS RELATED TO ROUTING

Objectives

Your router needs a routing table to route packets correctly and efficiently. Routing is an extremely important topic and an entire Cisco CCNP exam is devoted to it. At your current level, however, you only need to understand the basic concepts and terminology involved with routing. Learning those concepts and terminology are the objectives of this lab. You will match the bulleted routing terms in the activity with the definitions in Table 8-1.

After completing this lab you will:

> Understand the terms and concepts related to routing

Materials Required

This lab requires the following:

> Pencil or pen

Estimated completion time: **20 minutes**

ACTIVITY

1. Relate the following bulleted terms to the descriptions in Table 8-1 by placing them in the correct cell in the second column. There may be more than one term or phrase for each description. Each term is used at least once.

- Link-state
- Metric
- EGP
- Hold-down timers
- BGP
- Set a maximum

- Static
- Split horizon
- RIP
- Direct connection
- IGP
- Split horizon with poison reverse

- Administrative distance
- Distance-vector
- Convergence
- OSPF
- IGRP
- Nonroutable

- NetBEUI
- IPX
- EIGRP
- Autonomous system
- IP
- Routable

Table 8-1   Routing concepts and terminology

Routing Concept Description	Matching Term
Protocols that cannot be routed	
Protocols that broadcast their entire routing tables periodically	
A type of route used in a stub situation or as a backup	
The method a router uses to rank the reliability of routing information	
A group of routers that will share routing information and that are under the control of one administrator	
Protocols that can be routed	
Used to combat the count-to-infinity problem	
Protocols that, after the initial flooding of routing information, update neighbors at triggered intervals and consume relatively low bandwidth	
A method of determining the suitability of a route	
Routing protocols used within an autonomous system or private internetwork	
A state where all routers in the internetwork have a common view of the topology	
Administrative distance of 100 or less	
Non-proprietary commonly used routing protocol with a 15-hop limitation	
Routing protocols that can be used only between Cisco routers	
Routing protocols used between autonomous systems or private internetworks	

Certification Objectives

Objectives for the CCNA exam:

➤ List problems that each routing type encounters when dealing with topology changes, and describe techniques to reduce the number of these problems

Review Questions

1. A default route is a type of static route. What is it used for?

2. Why is it important to configure the same autonomous system number on all IGRP routers in your internetwork?

3. Rank IGRP, EIGRP, RIP, OSPF, static route, and direct connection in terms of administrative distance from lowest to highest. Record the administrative distance for each.

4. What is the difference between split horizon and split horizon with poison reverse?

LAB 8.2 CONFIGURE STATIC ROUTES

Objectives

The objective of this lab is to configure a static route on the router. To configure a router, you need to configure the interfaces and provide some way for the router to find routes to other routers. The two methods for finding routes are (1) to let the routers update one another through dynamic routing protocols, and (2) to statically configure the routes using the IP route command.

In this lab you will configure the router for a static route to a remote network. In the process of configuring the router, you will also learn about the show commands that are useful for monitoring network routes.

After completing this lab you will:

➤ Understand the command syntax for configuring static routing

➤ Know how to check the router for routing table information

➤ Be familiar with the output from the show ip route command

Materials Required

This lab requires the following:

➤ The internetworking lab setup as shown in Figure 8-1

➤ The successful completion of the labs in Chapter 6 and Lab 7.1

Estimated completion time: **30 minutes**

ACTIVITY

1. Start the computer with Windows and begin the HyperTerminal session with the router.

2. Turn on the router and hubs, if necessary. Press **Enter**, type the password **cisco** to get to the user EXEC mode prompt, type **ena**, and then press **Enter** to access privileged EXEC mode.

3. Type **class**, and then press **Enter** when prompted for the enable secret password.

4. Enter the **show interfaces** command and make sure the status of all the participating interfaces is up/up.

5. Type **show ip route**, and then press **Enter** to see the routing table information on the router. Which networks are directly connected to your router?

How do you know whether a network is directly connected?

Are there any networks your router has learned about through the RIP routing protocol?

How do you know whether a network has been learned about through RIP?

---

6. To configure a static route on a router, you must know the destination network number, the subnet mask, and the IP address of the next router interface (hop) in the path to the destination network. Review the syntax for the ip route command, which is shown here:

ip route [*remote network*] [*subnet mask*] [*ip address of interface on next hop in the path*] [*administrative distance* (optional)]

7. Examine the network in Figure 8-1. The following command configures a static route to network 205.7.5.0 from the lab-e router:

ip route 205.7.5.0 255.255.255.0 210.93.105.1 255

8

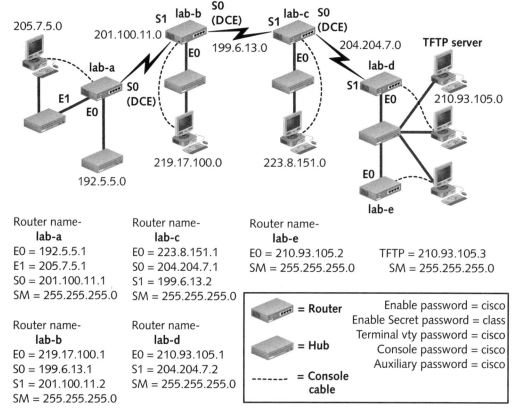

Figure 8-1 Connection information

8. The last IP address in the command in Step 7 is the E0 interface on the lab-d router. It corresponds to the next hop on the path to the destination network. The 255 at the end of the command is the optional administrative distance. If you don't put an administrative distance in the command, what is the default?

_____

9. Type **conf t**, and then press **Enter** to enter global configuration mode.

10. Use the **ip route** command to configure a static route on your router. Use an administrative distance of 255. Do not configure a static route to a network to which you are directly connected. Which router are you configuring?

_____

For which network are you configuring a static route?

_____

Which command did you enter?

_____

11. Use the **ip route** command to configure another static route on your router to a different remote network. Use an administrative distance of 255.

For which network are you configuring a static route?

_____

Which command did you enter?

_____

12. Press **Ctrl+Z** to return to the enable prompt, and then press **Enter** to clear the message.

13. Type **show ip route**, and then press **Enter** to see the routing table information on the router. Do you see your static routes? Why not?

_____

_____

14. Return to global configuration mode, and use the up arrow to find your static route commands. For each of them, remove the administrative distance, but leave the rest of the command intact.

15. Press **Ctrl+Z** to return to the enable prompt, and then press **Enter** to clear the message.

16. Type **show ip route**, and then press **Enter** to see the routing table information on the router.

You should see your static routes. What is the symbol that lets you know these are static routes?

_____

Why did removing the administrative distance of 255 from the static route commands change the routing table in this way?

_____

_____

17. Do not save the configuration. Type **logout**, and then press **Enter** to exit the router.

Certification Objectives

Objectives for the CCNA exam:

➤ This lab does not map to a certification objective; however, it contains information that will be beneficial to your professional development

Review Questions

1. What is a stub router?

2. Why do you think the administrative distance of a static route is only 1?

3. What is the purpose of changing the default administrative distance of a static route?

4. What is the only type of routing table entry that would have a default administrative distance less then the default administrative distance of a static route?

LAB 8.3 CONFIGURE RIP

Objectives

The objective of this lab is to demonstrate how to configure the router for RIP. RIP is the most common dynamic routing protocol in use on smaller internetworks. In this lab you will configure the router for the RIP dynamic routing protocol. In addition, you will change the timer information including the update interval. You will also use the show commands and a debug command for monitoring network routes.

After completing this lab you will:

➤ Understand the difference between dynamic routing and static routing

➤ Understand the command syntax for configuring RIP routing

➤ Be familiar with the output from the show ip protocols, show ip route, and debug ip rip commands

Materials Required

This lab requires the following:

➤ The successful completion of the labs in Chapter 6 and Lab 7.1

➤ The internetworking lab setup shown in Figure 8-1

Estimated completion time: **30 minutes**

ACTIVITY

1. Start the computer with Windows and begin the HyperTerminal session with the router.

2. Turn on the router, if necessary. Press **Enter**, type the password **cisco** to get to the user EXEC mode prompt, type **ena**, and then press **Enter** to access privileged EXEC mode.

3. Type **class**, and then press **Enter** when prompted for the enable secret password.

4. Enter global configuration mode.

5. Remove RIP from the router using the **no router rip** command.

6. Type **Ctrl+Z** to return to enable mode.

7. Wait a few minutes for the RIP routes to be flushed from the router.

8. Type **show ip route**, and then press **Enter**. Are all of your routes either directly connected or statically configured?

_____

_____

If the answer is "no" and RIP routes are still active, wait a few more seconds and try the **show ip route** command again. You should proceed to Step 9 only when you have confirmed that no RIP routes are active.

9. Enter global configuration mode.

10. Type **router rip** to enter router configuration mode.

11. Now enter the networks to which your router is directly connected. Refer back to Figure 8-1, and use the **network** command to indicate which networks are directly connected to your router. For example, if you are configuring the lab-d router, you are directly connected to networks 204.204.7.0 and 210.93.105.0. In this case, you would type:

network 204.204.7.0 [Enter]

network 210.93.105.0 [Enter]

12. Press **Ctrl+Z** to return to the enable prompt, press **Enter** to clear the message, and then wait a minute to give the router a chance to update its routing table.

13. Type **show ip route**, and then press **Enter**. Has your router obtained any route information via RIP?

_____

14. Type **show ip protocol**, and then press **Enter**. What is the RIP update interval?

_____

What is the invalid interval?

_____

What is the hold-down timer interval?

_____

What is the flush interval?

_____

15. Enter global configuration mode, then type **router rip** and press **Enter** to enter router configuration mode.

16. The timers basic command will allow you to change the default timers you recorded in Step 14. Review the format of the command below:

    timers basic [*update interval*] [*invalid interval*] [*hold-down timer*] [*flush interval*]

17. Type **timers basic 60 500 360 440** and press **Enter**.

18. Press **Ctrl+Z** to return to enable mode.

19. Type **show ip protocol** and review the timer information. Have the timers been reconfigured, as was shown by the commands in Step 17?

    _____

20. Type **debug ip rip**, and then press **Enter**. Watch the screen a minute or so to see the displayed information. What useful information can be obtained from this command?

    _____

21. Press **Enter** if necessary to get to the prompt, and then type **no debug all** and press **Enter** to disable all debugging.

22. Do not save the configuration. Type **logout**, and then press **Enter** to exit the router.

Certification Objectives

Objectives for the CCNA exam:

➤ Add the RIP routing protocol to your configuration.

Review Questions

1. What is an advantage of increasing the update interval?

2. What is the purpose of the hold-down timer?

3. List three commands to turn off the debugging you configured using the debug ip rip command.

4. What is the purpose of the flush interval?

LAB 8.4 CONFIGURE IGRP

Objectives

The objective of this lab is to configure the router for IGRP. IGRP is Cisco's answer to RIP. This proprietary, dynamic routing protocol uses bandwidth and delay as its primary metrics. In this lab you will configure the router for the IGRP dynamic routing protocol. You will also use the show ip protocol command and a debug command for monitoring network routes.

After completing this lab you will:

➤ Understand the difference between dynamic routing and static routing

➤ Understand the command syntax for configuring IGRP routing

➤ Know how to check the router for routing table information

➤ Be familiar with the output from the show ip protocols and debug ip igrp events commands

Materials Required

This lab requires the following:

➤ The successful completion of the labs in Chapter 6 and Lab 7.1

➤ The internetworking lab setup as shown in Figure 8-1

Estimated completion time: **30 minutes**

ACTIVITY

1. Start the computer with Windows and begin the HyperTerminal session with the router.

2. Turn on the router, if necessary. Press **Enter**, type the password **cisco** to get to the user EXEC mode prompt, type **ena**, and then press **Enter** to access privileged EXEC mode.

3. Type **class**, and then press **Enter** when prompted for the enable secret password.

4. Enter global configuration mode.

5. Type **no router rip**, and then press **Enter** to disable RIP.

6. Type **router igrp 100**, and then press **Enter** to enable IGRP. To what did the prompt change?

_____

What does the number 100 represent?

_____

7. Refer back to Figure 8-1 and use the **network [*network #*]** command to enable IGRP routing for the networks that are directly connected to your router.

8. Type **Ctrl+Z** to return to enable mode.

9. Type **show ip protocol**, and then press **Enter**. Is IGRP configured on the router?

_____

What is the update interval?

_____

What is the invalid interval?

_____

What is the hold-down timer interval?

_____

What is the flush interval?

_____

10. Type **show ip route** and press **Enter**. Are there any IGRP routes indicated?

_____

If the answer is no, what is your explanation?

_____

_____

11. Type **debug ip igrp events**, and then press **Enter**. Watch the screen a minute or so to see the displayed information. What useful information can be obtained from this command?

_____

_____

_____

12. Type **no debug all**, and then press **Enter** to disable all debugging.

13. Do not save the configuration. Type **reload**, and then press **Enter** to reboot the router. Press **n** for no and then **Enter** if you are asked to save the configuration. Confirm the reload if necessary.

Certification Objectives

Objectives for the CCNA exam:

> ➤ Add the IGRP routing protocol to your configuration

Review Questions

1. Can IGRP be used on non–Cisco routers? Why or why not?

2. Why do routers running distance-vector routing protocols such as RIP and IGRP take a relatively long time to converge?

3. If debug is so informative, why not leave it on all the time for monitoring purposes?

4. What is the advantage of having a longer update interval?

8

CHAPTER NINE

IPX/SPX

Labs included in this chapter

➤ Lab 9.1 Configure IPX

➤ Lab 9.2 Configure IPX Subinterfaces

➤ Lab 9.3 Monitor IPX/SPX

➤ Lab 9.4 Understanding Frame Types and Cisco Encapsulations

CCNA Exam Objectives

Objective	Lab
Describe the two parts of network addressing; then identify the parts in specific protocol address examples	9.1, 9.3
List the required IPX address and encapsulation type	9.1, 9.2, 9.4

LAB 9.1 CONFIGURE IPX

Objectives

The objective of this lab is to understand the two-step process involved in configuring IPX on a Cisco router. This process includes enabling IPX on the router and then configuring the interfaces with IPX network numbers and appropriate encapsulations. In this lab you will enable IPX routing on a router and configure IPX on all interfaces of that router in the internetworking lab.

After completing this lab you will be able to:

➤ Enable IPX on a router

➤ Configure IPX on all router interfaces

Materials Required

This lab requires the following:

➤ The internetworking lab setup used in the labs in Chapters 6, 7, and 8

➤ The successful completion of the labs in Chapter 6 and Lab 7.1

Estimated completion time: **45 minutes**

ACTIVITY

1. Turn on the workstation and open the HyperTerminal program on each workstation that will connect to the routers.

2. Turn on the routers and hubs, if necessary.

3. Press **Enter** on the workstations if you need to initiate a response from the router.

4. Log into the router using the console password **cisco** and the enable password **class**. Which router are you configuring?

_____

5. Enter global configuration mode.

6. Enable the router for IPX using the **ipx routing** command.

7. Enter interface configuration mode for an interface on your router. The IPX network numbers and their corresponding NetWare frame format designations are shown in Figure 9-1.

8. Configure the interface for IPX by using the **ipx network [*network number*] encap [*cisco encapsulation*]** command. The Cisco encapsulations are not shown in Figure 9-1. You will have to configure the correct encapsulations based on the NetWare frame format designations shown in the figure.

Remember that HDLC is the default Cisco encapsulation on serial interfaces. Therefore, you do not need to add the encapsulation for the serial interfaces. You only need the network number portion of the command.

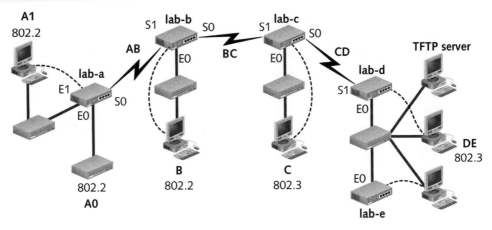

Figure 9-1   IPX configuration information

9

9. Continue configuring IPX on all router interfaces used by the router you are configuring, per Figure 9-1. Which IPX commands did you enter on which interfaces?

_____

_____

_____

10. Return to enable mode by pressing **Ctrl+Z**.

11. Display the running configuration. How can you verify the router is configured for IPX?

_____

There should be an address listed after the words "ipx routing" in the running configuration file. What do you think this address represents?

_____

_____

Are IP and IPX configured on every connected interface?

_____

If IP and IPX are not configured on every connected interface, configure the unconfigured interfaces.

12. Use the **show ipx interface** command to display IPX interface information. What is the entire IPX address of each interface on your router?

_____

_____

_____

What is the SAP update interval?

_____

What is the RIP update interval?

_____

13. Copy the running configuration to the startup configuration.

14. Log out of the router.

Certification Objectives

Objectives for the CCNA exam:

➤ Describe the two parts of network addressing; then identify the parts in specific protocol address examples

➤ List the required IPX address and encapsulation type

Review Questions

1. What is the difference between IP RIP and IPX RIP?

2. Is the ip routing command necessary to enable IP? Why or why not?

3. How do you think you could disable IPX routing on a router?

4. The MAC address is part of an IPX address. If all MAC addresses are unique, why do serial interfaces on the router have the same MAC addresses as an Ethernet interface on a router, as illustrated using the show ipx interface command in Step 12 of this lab?

LAB 9.2 CONFIGURE IPX SUBINTERFACES

Objectives

The objective of this lab is to configure IPX using subinterfaces and the subinterface configuration mode. In this lab you will configure IPX on the Ethernet subinterfaces shown in Figure 9-2. After verifying that the running configuration matches the desired setup, you will copy the new running configuration to the startup configuration.

After completing this lab you will be able to:

➤ Configure IPX on Ethernet subinterfaces

Materials Required

This lab requires the following:

➤ The internetworking lab setup used in the labs in Chapters 6, 7, and 8

➤ The successful completion of the labs in Chapter 6, Lab 7.1, and Lab 9.1

9

Estimated completion time: **30 minutes**

ACTIVITY

1. If necessary, turn on the workstations.

2. Open the HyperTerminal program on each workstation that will connect to the routers.

3. If necessary, turn on the routers and hubs.

4. Press **Enter** on the workstations if you need to initiate a response from the router.

5. Enter enable mode using **cisco** as the console password and **class** as the enable password.

6. Enter global configuration mode.

7. Type **int e0.1**, and then press **Enter** to put the router into subinterface mode. What did the prompt change to?

_____

Examine the IPX subinterface information for the internetworking lab shown in Figure 9-2. The Ethernet subinterfaces with their corresponding network numbers are shown. Notice that all encapsulations should be configured for the Ethernet_II frame type.

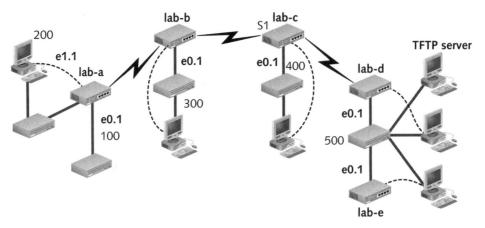

Figure 9-2   IPX subinterface configuration information

8. Configure an Ethernet subinterface for your router for IPX using the **ipx network** [*network number*] **encap** [*cisco encapsulation*] command. The lab-a router has two Ethernet interfaces, so two separate commands will be necessary on this router, one for e0.1 and one for e1.1. Which IPX command(s) did you enter?

_____

9. Return to enable mode by pressing **Ctrl+Z**.

10. Display the running configuration. Are the Ethernet interfaces and subinterfaces configured correctly?

_____

If the interfaces are not configured correctly per Figure 9-1 and 9-2, reconfigure the interfaces.

11. Copy the running configuration to the startup configuration.

12. Log out of the router.

Certification Objectives

Objectives for the CCNA exam:

➤ List the required IPX address and encapsulation type

Review Questions

1. Why is it important to be able to use subinterfaces on a router?

2. What is the benefit of using subinterfaces rather than the secondary command?

3. How do you create a subinterface?

LAB 9.3 MONITOR IPX/SPX

Objectives

The objective of this lab is to monitor the newly configured routers from Labs 9.1 and 9.2 by using the show ipx route, show ipx traffic, ping, and the debug ipx routing activity commands.

The show ipx route command displays the current IPX routing table contained on a router. It will enable you to determine whether the routers know about other IPX networks. The show ipx traffic command displays information about the number and type of IPX packets sent and received. The ping command operates as it does for IP, verifying Network layer connectivity between hosts. The debug ipx routing activity command enables you to monitor IPX traffic across the router in real time. Specifically, the debug ipx routing activity command turns on debugging for RIP and NLSP routing updates. In this lab you will use these commands to monitor your IPX configurations.

After completing this lab you will be able to:

➤ Use the show ipx route, show ipx traffic, ping, and debug ipx routing activity commands

➤ Extract important information from the output of the show ipx route and debug ipx routing activity commands

Materials Required

This lab requires the following:

➤ The internetworking lab setup used in the labs in Chapters 6, 7, and 8

➤ The successful completion of the labs in Chapter 6, Lab 7.1, and Labs 9.1 and 9.2

Estimated completion time: **15 minutes**

ACTIVITY

1. If necessary, turn on the workstations.

2. Open the HyperTerminal program on each workstation that will connect to the routers.

3. If necessary, turn on the routers and hubs.

4. Press **Enter** on the workstations if you need to initiate a response from the router.

5. Enter enable mode using **cisco** as the console password and **class** as the enable password.

6. Type the **show ipx route** command, and then press **Enter**. If there are no routes in the table, make sure the status of your interfaces is up/up and that your teammates have configured IPX on their routers. Which router are you examining?

_____

Which IPX networks are directly connected to your router?

_____

_____

_____

Which IPX networks did the router learn about via RIP?

_____

_____

_____

What is the default Cisco encapsulation on serial interfaces?

_____

7. Ping an IPX interface that you recorded in Lab 9.1, Step 12, by using the **ping ipx [*ipx address*]** command. Make sure that you use the entire IPX address. Was the ping operation successful?

_____

If not, try pinging a different IPX interface.

8. Type **show ipx traffic** and press **Enter**. What important information can be ascertained from this command output?

_____

_____

9. Turn debugging on using the **debug ipx routing activity** command. Wait a minute for debugging to appear on your screen. IPX RIP information should be displayed. How can you tell that RIP uses broadcasts to update neighboring routers?

_____

_____

10. Turn debugging off by using the **no debug ipx routing activity** command.

11. Log out of the router.

Certification Objectives

Objectives for the CCNA exam:

➤ Describe the two parts of network addressing; then identify the parts in specific protocol address examples

Review Questions

1. What is the difference between show ipx traffic and debug ipx routing activity command output?

2. Why do MAC addresses appear in an IPX routing table, but not in an IP routing table?

3. Why is no encapsulation configuration necessary for 802.3 networks or serial interfaces?

9

4. What show command displays the SAP entries in a router?

LAB 9.4 UNDERSTANDING FRAME TYPES AND CISCO ENCAPSULATIONS

Objectives

As you know from previous labs, in order for Cisco routers to participate in IPX/SPX networks, their interfaces must use the same encapsulation type as the networks to which they are attached. The objective of this lab is to make sure you have memorized Novell frame format designations and their corresponding network operating systems and Cisco encapsulation terminologies.

After completing this lab you will be able to:

➤ Understand the Novell NetWare frame format designations and their corresponding network operating systems

➤ Understand Cisco encapsulation terminology

Materials Required

This lab requires the following:

➤ Pencil or pen

Estimated completion time: **15 minutes**

ACTIVITY

1. In Table 9-1, fill in the blank cells with the correct network operating system versions, Novell frame format designations, and Cisco encapsulation terminology.

Table 9-1   IPX/SPX encapsulation information

Network Operating System	Novell Frame Format	Cisco Encapsulation
NetWare version 3.11 or lower		
	802.2	
		Arpa
IPX/SPX, TCP/IP, and AppleTalk		

Certification Objectives

Objectives for the CCNA exam:

➤ List the required IPX address and encapsulation type

Review Questions

1. Cisco routers support Novell frame type designations, as discussed in this lab. What other Novell frame type designations do the routers cover that are *not* discussed in this lab?

2. What frame format would you use for a network using both NetWare and NT servers?

3. What frame format would you use for a token ring network?

4. What frame format would you use for a network using both AppleTalk and TCP/IP?

ACCESS LISTS

10

Labs included in this chapter

➤ Lab 10.1 Create and Apply a Standard IP Access List on the Lab-d Router

➤ Lab 10.2 Create and Apply an Extended IP Access List on the Lab-b Router

➤ Lab 10.3 Create and Apply a Standard IPX Access List on the Lab-c Router

➤ Lab 10.4 Create and Apply an Extended IPX Access List on the Lab-a Router

➤ Lab 10.5 Create and Apply a SAP Filter on the Lab-e Router

CCNA Exam Objectives	
Objective	**Lab**
Configure standard access lists to filter IP traffic	10.1
Configure extended access lists to filter IP traffic	10.2
Monitor and verify selected access list operations on the router	10.1, 10.2, 10.3, 10.4, 10.5

LAB 10.1 CREATE AND APPLY A STANDARD IP ACCESS LIST ON THE LAB-D ROUTER

Objectives

The objective of this lab is to configure a standard IP access list, which filters traffic based on source IP addresses. This process is carried out in two steps. First, the list is created using a text editor and configured in global configuration mode. Second, the list is applied to the appropriate interface as either an inbound list or an outbound list in interface configuration mode.

In this lab, you will create a standard IP access list that will deny access to network 210.93.105.0 from any host on network 205.7.5.0. You then will apply it to the appropriate interface on the lab-d router in the internetworking lab. Finally, you will monitor and test your list.

Note that it is important that you complete the first six questions of this lab before attempting to configure the router. This will save time because designing the list is the most time-consuming part of the access list configuration process and can be done in advance.

After completing this lab you will be able to:

➤ Create a standard IP access list using Notepad

➤ Configure the standard IP access list and apply it to the appropriate interface

➤ Use the correct show commands to monitor the standard IP access list

➤ Test the standard IP access list

Materials Required

This lab requires the following:

➤ The internetworking lab setup used in the labs from Chapters 6, 7, 8, and 9 labs

➤ The successful completion of the labs in Chapters 6, 7, and 9

Estimated completion time: **45 minutes**

ACTIVITY

Do not skip the first six questions in this lab. Doing so will only slow down the configuration process.

1. Examine Figure 10-1. The access list to deny access to network 210.93.105.0 from any host on network 205.7.5.0 should be created and applied on the lab-d router. Why?

_____

_____

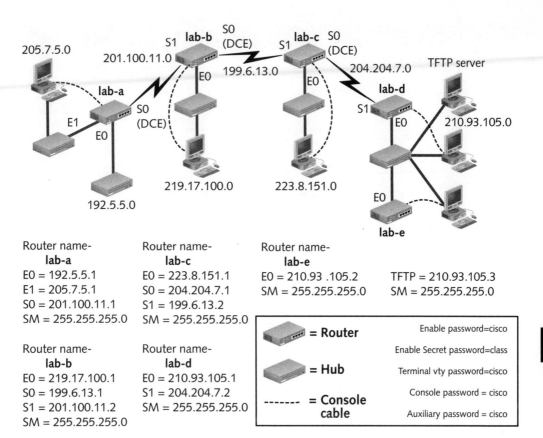

Router name-
lab-a
E0 = 192.5.5.1
E1 = 205.7.5.1
S0 = 201.100.11.1
SM = 255.255.255.0

Router name-
lab-c
E0 = 223.8.151.1
S0 = 204.204.7.1
S1 = 199.6.13.2
SM = 255.255.255.0

Router name-
lab-e
E0 = 210.93 .105.2
SM = 255.255.255.0

TFTP = 210.93.105.3
SM = 255.255.255.0

Router name-
lab-b
E0 = 219.17.100.1
S0 = 199.6.13.1
S1 = 201.100.11.2
SM = 255.255.255.0

Router name-
lab-d
E0 = 210.93.105.1
S1 = 204.204.7.2
SM = 255.255.255.0

= **Router**	Enable password=cisco
	Enable Secret password=class
= **Hub**	Terminal vty password=cisco
	Console password = cisco
------- = **Console cable**	Auxiliary password = cisco

Figure 10-1   Connection information

2. Write the access list to deny any traffic from network 205.7.5.0 from reaching any host on network 210.93.105.0. Don't forget the permit statement. Use Figure 10-1 for reference.

_____

_____

3. Why is the permit statement necessary?

_____

_____

4. Which list number did you use in the list?

_____

What is the acceptable range for a standard IP list?

_____

Correct your list number in Step 2, if necessary.

10

5. On which interface and in which direction will you apply the list you created in Step 2?

_____

Why?

_____

_____

6. Which command will you use to apply the access list?

_____

7. Turn on the Windows computers, routers, and hubs, if necessary. Attach a UTP patch cable between the NIC card in the lab-a Windows computer and the hub connected to the E1 interface of the lab-a router. Make sure the NIC light on the computer and the corresponding port light on the hub are on.

8. Right-click **Network Neighborhood** on the lab-a Windows computer. Make sure the IP address and gateway configured on the computer are 205.7.5.2 and 205.7.5.1, respectively. You may have to restart the computer if you make any IP configuration changes to the workstation.

9. Return to the lab-d computer, if necessary. Log into the lab-d router using **cisco** as the console password. Enter enable mode using the password **class**.

10. Enter global configuration mode.

11. Click the Windows **Start** button, point to **Programs**, point to **Accessories**, and then click **Notepad** to open the Notepad program.

12. Type **no access-list [#]**, where [#] is the list number that you recorded in Step 4. Press **Enter**. Why should this statement be the first line in your text editor access list?

_____

_____

13. Type the access list commands created in Step 2 on separate lines under the no access-list command.

14. Highlight and copy your list to the Clipboard.

15. Minimize Notepad, right-click beside the **lab-d (config)#** prompt, and then click **Paste to Host**. Your list should be entered into the router's running configuration. If it didn't work, try the copy-and-paste operation again.

16. When will the access list take effect?

_____

_____

17. Enter interface configuration mode for the interface you specified in Step 5.

18. Apply the list using the command you specified in Step 6.

19. Press **Ctrl+Z** to return to enable mode.

20. Use the **show access-lists** command to see the access list defined on the lab-d router. What information is provided by this command?

    _____

21. In this case, which other command will give you identical information?

    _____

22. Type **show ip interface**, and then press **Enter**. What kind of information do you get regarding the access list?

    _____

23. Move to the computer attached to the lab-a router or ask your teammate configuring the lab-a router to do the next three steps for you. Make sure that it is turned on and close any open programs, if necessary.

24. Shell out to DOS by clicking **Start**, pointing to **Programs**, and then clicking **MS-DOS**.

25. Type **ping 210.93.105.2**, and then press **Enter**.

26. What was the response?

    _____

    What does the response mean?

    _____

    _____

27. If you were able to ping successfully, your access list is incorrect or is applied incorrectly. Make any necessary corrections to your access list in Notepad, copy and paste to the host again, and then retest.

28. Close the DOS window on the workstation connected to the lab-a router.

29. Return to the lab-d router, if necessary.

30. Enter global configuration mode then interface configuration mode for the interface on which the list is applied.

31. Use the **no ip access-group [#] [*direction*]** command, where # is the list number and *direction* is either in or out, to remove the list from the interface.

32. Type **exit** to return to global configuration mode.

33. Type **no access-list [#]**, where # is the list number, to remove the list from the router.

34. Exit to enable mode and use the **show access-lists** command to verify that the list has been removed.

35. Log out of the lab-d router.

10

Certification Objectives

Objectives for the CCNA exam:

➤ Configure standard access lists to filter IP traffic.

➤ Monitor and verify selected access list operations on the router.

Review Questions

1. How does using Notepad facilitate creating access lists in the router?

2. Why must standard IP access lists be applied as close to the destination as possible?

3. What is the wildcard mask that filters any host on a class B network?

4. What is the wildcard mask that filters any host on a class A network?

LAB 10.2 CREATE AND APPLY AN EXTENDED IP ACCESS LIST ON THE LAB-B ROUTER

Objectives

The objective of this lab is to configure an extended IP access list. This process is the same as that for a standard IP access list. First, the list is created using a text editor and configured in global configuration mode. Second, it is applied to the appropriate interface as either an inbound list or an outbound list in interface configuration mode.

In this lab you will create an extended IP access list to deny the host with the IP address 219.17.100.2 from pinging the host with IP address 205.7.5.2. You will then apply the list to the appropriate interface on the lab-b router in the internetworking lab. Finally, you will monitor and test your list.

Note that it is important that you complete the first six questions of this lab before attempting to configure the router. This will save time because designing the list is the most time-consuming part of the access list configuration process and can be done in advance.

After completing this lab you will be able to:

> ➤ Create an extended IP access list using Notepad

> ➤ Configure the extended IP access list and apply it to the appropriate interface

> ➤ Use the correct show commands to monitor the extended IP access list

> ➤ Test the extended IP access list

Materials Required

This lab requires the following:

> ➤ The internetworking lab setup used in the Chapters 6, 7, 8, and 9 labs

> ➤ The successful completion of the labs in Chapters 6, 7, and 9

> ➤ Two extra UTP patch cables

Estimated completion time: **45 minutes**

ACTIVITY

Do not skip the first six questions in this lab. Doing so will only slow down the configuration process.

1. Examine Figure 10-1 again. The access list to deny the host with the IP address 219.17.100.2 from pinging the host with IP address 205.7.5.2 should be created and applied on the lab-b router. Why?

   _____

   _____

2. Write the access list to deny ping traffic from node 219.17.100.2 from reaching host 205.7.5.2. Do not forget the permit statement. Use Figure 10-1 for reference.

   _____

   _____

3. Why is the permit statement necessary?

   _____

   _____

4. Which list number did you use in the list?

   _____

   What is the acceptable range for an extended IP list?

   _____

   Correct your list number in Step 2, if necessary.

10

5. On which interface and in which direction will you apply the list you created in Step 2?

_____

Why?

_____

_____

6. Which command will you use to apply the access list?

_____

7. Turn on the Windows computers, routers, and hubs, if necessary. Make sure a UTP patch cable is between the NIC card in the lab-a Windows computer and the hub connected to the E1 interface of the lab-a router. Make sure the NIC light on the computer and the corresponding port light on the hub are on. The lab-b computer should be attached via UTP to the hub connected to the E0 interface on the lab-b router. Again, check lights to make sure you have physical layer connectivity.

8. Right-click **Network Neighborhood** on the lab-a Windows computer. Make sure the IP address and gateway configured on the computer are 205.7.5.2 and 205.7.5.1, respectively. You may have to restart the computer if you changed the IP configuration of the workstation.

9. Right-click **Network Neighborhood** on the lab-b Windows computer. Make sure the IP address and gateway configured on the computer are 219.17.100.2 and 219.17.100.1, respectively. You may have to restart the computer if you changed the IP configuration of the workstation.

10. Return to the lab-b computer if necessary. Shell out to the MS-DOS prompt using the **Start**, **Programs**, and **MS-DOS Prompt** menus.

11. Type **ping 205.7.5.2**, and then press **Enter**.

What was the response?

_____

What does the response mean?

_____

_____

12. If you were unable to ping successfully, start troubleshooting with the help of your instructor. Make sure all of the interfaces between the lab-b router and the lab-a router have an up/up status. After you can ping successfully, continue with the next step.

13. Close the DOS window on the workstation connected to the lab-b router.

14. Log into the lab-b router using **cisco** as the console password. Enter enable mode using the password **class**.

15. Enter global configuration mode.

16. Click the Windows **Start** button, point to **Programs**, point to **Accessories**, and then click **Notepad** to open the Notepad program.

17. Type **no access-list [#]**, where [#] is the list number that you recorded in Step 4, and then press **Enter**. Why should this statement be the first line in your text editor access list?

    _____

    _____

18. Type the access list commands created in Step 2 on separate lines under the no access-list command.

19. Highlight and copy your list to the Clipboard.

20. Minimize Notepad, right-click beside the **lab-b (config)#** prompt, and then click **Paste to Host**. Your list should be entered into the router's running configuration.

21. When will the access list take effect?

    _____

    _____

22. Enter interface configuration mode for the interface you specified in Step 5.

23. Apply the list using the command you specified in Step 6.

24. Press **Ctrl+Z** to return to enable mode.

25. Shell out to the MS-DOS prompt using the **Start**, **Programs**, and **MS-DOS Prompt** menus.

26. Type **ping 205.7.5.2**, and then press **Enter**.

27. What was the response?

    _____

    What does the response mean?

    _____

    _____

28. If you were able to ping successfully, your access list is incorrect or applied incorrectly. Make any necessary corrections to your access list in Notepad, copy and paste to host again, and then retest.

29. Close the DOS window on the workstation connected to the lab-b router.

30. Use the **show access-lists** command to see the access list defined on the lab-b router. What information is provided by this command?

    _____

10

31. Compared to using this command with a standard IP list, what additional information do you receive for an extended IP list? (*Hint*: matches)

_____

_____

32. Type **clear access-list counters [#]**, where # is the list number, and then press **Enter**. What do you think this command does?

_____

33. Use the **show access-lists** command again. Were the counters (matches) cleared?

_____

34. Enter global configuration mode and then interface configuration mode for the interface on which the list is applied.

35. Use the **no ip access-group [#] [*direction*]** command, where # is the list number and *direction* is either in or out, to remove the list from the interface.

36. Type **exit** to return to global configuration mode.

37. Type **no access-list [#]**, where # is the list number, to remove the list from the router.

38. Exit to enable mode and use the **show access-lists** command to verify that the list has been removed.

39. Log out of the lab-b router.

Certification Objectives

Objectives for the CCNA exam:

➤ Configure extended access lists to filter IP traffic

➤ Monitor and verify selected access list operations on the router

Review Questions

1. What does the host keyword represent?

2. What does the any keyword represent?

3. With standard IP lists, the 0.0.0.0 wildcard mask is assumed. Is it also assumed with extended IP lists?

LAB 10.3 CREATE AND APPLY A STANDARD IPX ACCESS LIST ON THE LAB-C ROUTER

Objectives

The objective of this lab is to configure a standard IPX access list. This process is the same as that for a standard IP access list. The only difference is that a standard IPX list includes both the source and the destination addresses. In this lab, you will create a standard IPX access list in global configuration mode. The list should deny all traffic from network 400 from reaching network A1. You will then apply the list to the appropriate interface on the lab-c router. Finally, you will monitor the list.

Note that it is important that you complete the first six questions of this lab before attempting to configure the router. This will save time because designing the list is the most time-consuming part of the access list configuration process and can be done in advance.

After completing this lab you will be able to:

➤ Create a standard IPX access list in global configuration mode

➤ Apply the standard IPX access list to the appropriate interface

➤ Use the correct show commands to monitor the standard IPX access list

10

Materials Required

This lab requires the following:

➤ The internetworking lab setup used in the labs from Chapters 6, 7, 8, and 9

➤ The successful completion of the labs in Chapters 6, 7, and 9

Estimated completion time: **30 minutes**

ACTIVITY

Do not skip the first six questions in this lab. Doing so will only slow down the configuration process.

1. The access list to deny all traffic from network 400 from reaching network A1 should be created and applied on the lab-c router. Why?

_____

_____

2. Use Figures 10-2 and 10-3 to identify the location of networks 400 and A1. Write the access list to deny all traffic from network 400 from reaching network A1. Don't forget the permit statement.

_____

_____

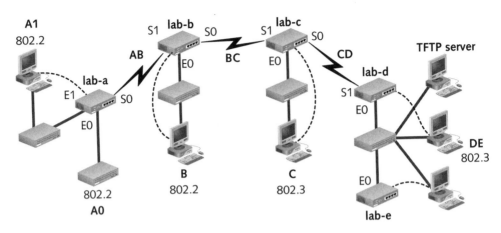

Figure 10-2   IPX configuration information

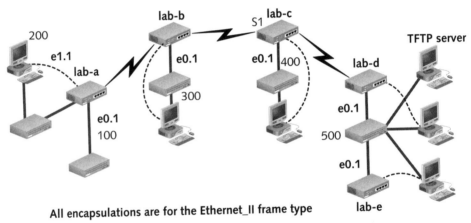

All encapsulations are for the Ethernet_II frame type

Figure 10-3   IPX subinterface configuration information

3. Why is the permit statement necessary?

_____

_____

4. Which list number did you use?

_____

What is the acceptable range for a standard IPX list?

_____

Correct your list number in Step 2, if necessary.

5. On which interface and in which direction will you apply the list you created
   in Step 2?

_____

Why?

_____

_____

6. Which command will you use to apply the access list?

_____

7. Log into the lab-c router using **cisco** as the console password. Enter enable mode using the password **class**.

8. Enter global configuration mode.

9. Click the Windows **Start** button, point to **Programs**, point to **Accessories**, and then click **Notepad** to open the Notepad program.

10. Type **no access-list [#]**, where [#] is the list number that you recorded in Step 4, and then press **Enter**. Why should this statement be the first line in your text editor access list?

_____

_____

11. Type the access list commands created in Step 2 on separate lines under the no access-list command.

12. Highlight and copy your list to the Clipboard.

13. Minimize Notepad, right-click beside the **lab–c (config)#** prompt, and then click **Paste to Host**. Your list should be entered into the router's running configuration.

14. When will the access list take effect?

_____

_____

15. Enter interface configuration mode for the interface you specified in Step 5.

16. Apply the list using the command you specified in Step 6.

17. Press **Ctrl+Z** to return to enable mode.

18. Use the **show access-lists** command to see the access list defined on the lab-c router. What information is provided by this command?

_____

19. Type **show ipx interface**, and then press **Enter**. What information did you receive from this command?

_____

20. Enter interface configuration mode for the interface on which the list is applied.

21. Use the **no ipx access-group [#] [_direction_]** command, where # is the list number and _direction_ is either in or out, to remove the list from the interface.

22. Type **exit** to return to global configuration mode.

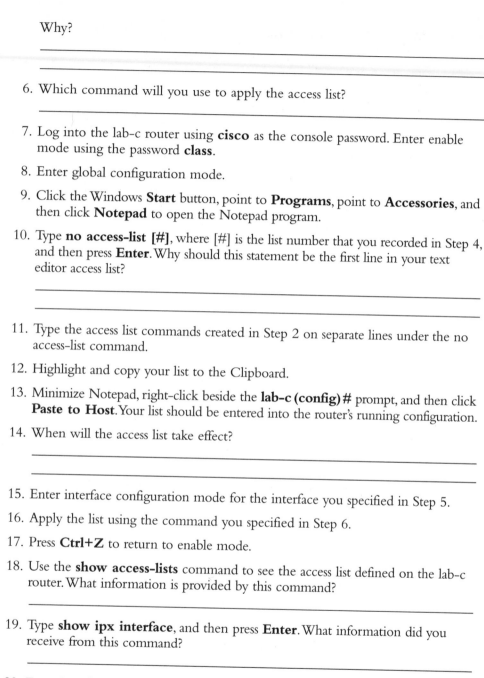

10

23. Type **no access-list [#]**, where # is the list number, to remove the list from the router.

24. Exit to enable mode and use the **show access-lists** command to verify that the list has been removed.

25. Log out of the lab-c router.

Certification Objectives

Objectives for the CCNA exam:

➤ Monitor and verify selected access list operations on the router

Review Questions

1. Why isn't the standard IPX list applied as close to the destination as possible, as is the case with the standard IP list?

2. What does the –1 represent in the permit statement?

3. Is it possible to specify the source and destination hosts and not just the source and destination networks in an IPX list? How would the list look?

Lab 10.4 Create and Apply an Extended IPX Access List on the Lab-a Router

Objectives

The objective of this lab is to configure an extended IPX access list. This process is much the same as that for a standard IPX access list. The difference is that an extended IPX list includes protocols and sockets as well as source and destination addresses. In this lab, you will create an extended IPX access list in global configuration mode. This list should deny (for all IPX protocols) all traffic from network A0 (on all sockets) from reaching network DE (on all sockets). You will then apply this list to the appropriate interface on the lab-a router. Finally, you will monitor the list.

Note that it is important that you complete the first six questions of this lab before attempting to configure the router. This will save time because designing the list is the most time-consuming part of the access list configuration process and can be done in advance.

After completing this lab you will be able to:

> ➤ Create an extended IPX access list using Notepad

> ➤ Configure the extended IPX access list and apply it to the appropriate interface

> ➤ Use the correct show commands to monitor the extended IPX access list

Materials Required

This lab requires the following:

> ➤ The internetworking lab setup used in the labs from Chapters 6, 7, 8, and 9

> ➤ The successful completion of the labs in Chapters 6, 7, and 9

Estimated completion time: **45 minutes**

ACTIVITY

Do not skip the first six questions in this lab. Doing so will only slow down the configuration process.

10

1. The access list to deny (for all IPX protocols) all traffic from network A0 (on all sockets) from reaching network DE (on all sockets) should be created and applied on the lab-a router. Why?

   _____

   _____

2. Write the access list to deny (for all IPX protocols) all traffic from network A0 (on all sockets) from reaching network DE (on all sockets). Do not forget the permit statement. Use Figure 10-2 to identify the location of networks A0 and DE.

   _____

   _____

3. Why is the permit statement necessary?

   _____

   _____

4. Which list number did you use?

   _____

   What is the acceptable range for an extended IPX list?

   _____

   Correct your list number in Step 2, if necessary.

5. On which interface and in which direction will you apply the list you created in Step 2?

_____

Why?

_____

_____

6. Which command will you use to apply the access list?

_____

7. Log into the lab-a router using **cisco** as the console password. Enter enable mode using the password **class**.

8. Enter global configuration mode.

9. Click the Windows **Start** button, point to **Programs**, point to **Accessories**, and then click **Notepad** to open the Notepad program.

10. Type **no access-list [#]**, where [#] is the list number that you recorded in Step 4, and then press **Enter**. Why should this statement be the first line in your text editor access list?

_____

_____

11. Type the access list commands created in Step 2 on separate lines below your no access-list command.

12. Highlight and copy your list to the Clipboard.

13. Minimize Notepad, right-click beside the **lab-a(config)#** prompt, and then click **Paste to Host**. Your list should be entered into the router's running configuration.

14. When will the access list take effect?

_____

_____

15. Enter interface configuration mode for the interface you specified in Step 5.

16. Apply the list using the command you specified in Step 6.

17. Press **Ctrl+Z** to return to enable mode.

18. Use the **show access-lists** command to see the access list defined on the lab-a router. What information is provided by this command?

_____

19. Type **show ipx interface**, and then press **Enter**. What information did you receive from this command?

_____

20. Enter global configuration mode then interface configuration mode for the interface on which the list is applied.

21. Use the **no ipx access-group [#]** [*direction*] command, where # is the list number and *direction* is either in or out, to remove the list from the interface.

22. Type **exit** to return to global configuration mode.

23. Type **no access-list [#]**, where # is the list number, to remove the list from the router.

24. Exit to enable mode and use the **show access-lists** command to verify that the list has been removed.

25. Log out of the lab-a router.

Certification Objectives

Objectives for the CCNA exam:

➤ Monitor and verify selected access list operations on the router

Review Questions

1. What two things does a –1 in an extended IPX list represent?

2. What does a 0 in an extended IPX list represent?

3. What is a socket?

4. In addition to the –1, what keyword can be used to represent all IPX protocols in an extended IPX list?

5. In addition to the 0, what keyword can be used to represent all sockets in an extended IPX list?

10

LAB 10.5 CREATE AND APPLY A SAP FILTER ON THE LAB-E ROUTER

Objectives

The objective of this lab is to configure an IPX SAP filter. A SAP filter is a form of access list that prevents SAP updates from being broadcast. SAP filters are created and applied much like other access lists. In this lab, you will create an IPX SAP filter that will deny the lab-e router from advertising all SAP services from network 500 to the rest of the internetwork. You will then apply this filter to the appropriate interface on the lab-e router. Then, you will monitor the filter.

Note that it is important that you complete the first six questions of this lab before attempting to configure the router. This will save time because designing the list is the most time-consuming part of the access list configuration process and can be done in advance.

After completing this lab you will be able to:

➤ Create a SAP filter using Notepad

➤ Configure the list then apply the list to the appropriate interface

➤ Use the correct show commands to monitor the list

Materials Required

This lab requires the following:

➤ The internetworking lab setup used in the labs from Chapters 6, 7, 8, and 9

➤ The successful completion of the labs in Chapters 6, 7, and 9

Estimated completion time: **30 minutes**

ACTIVITY

Do not skip the first six questions in this lab. Doing so will only slow down the configuration process.

1. The SAP filter should be created and applied on the lab-e router. Why?

   _____

   _____

2. Use Figure 10-3 to identify the location of network 500. Write the access list to deny the lab-e router from advertising SAP updates from network 500 to the rest of the internetwork. Don't forget the permit statement.

   _____

   _____

3. Why is the permit statement necessary?

_____

_____

4. Which list number did you use?

_____

What is the acceptable range for an IPX SAP filter?

_____

Correct your list number in Step 2, if necessary.

5. On which interface and in which direction will you apply the filter you created in Step 2?

_____

Why?

_____

_____

6. Which command will you use to apply the SAP filter?

_____

7. Log into the lab-e router using **cisco** as the console password. Enter enable mode using the password **class**.

8. Enter global configuration mode.

9. Click the Windows **Start** button, point to **Programs**, point to **Accessories**, and then click **Notepad** to open the Notepad program.

10. Type **no access-list [#]**, where [#] is the list number that you recorded in Step 4, and then press **Enter**. Why should this statement be the first line in your text editor access list?

_____

_____

11. Type the access list commands created in Step 2 on separate lines under the no access-list command.

12. Highlight and copy your list to the Clipboard.

13. Minimize Notepad, right-click beside the **lab-e (config)#** prompt, and then click **Paste to Host**. Your list should be entered into the router's running configuration.

14. When will the SAP filter take effect?

_____

_____

15. Enter interface configuration mode for the interface you specified in Step 5.

16. Apply the list using the command you specified in Step 6.

17. Press **Ctrl+Z** to return to enable mode.

18. Use the **show access-lists** command to see the access list defined on the lab-e router. What information is provided by this command?

_____

19. Type **show ipx interface**, and then press **Enter**. What information did you receive from this command?

_____

20. Enter global configuration mode and then interface configuration mode for the interface on which the filter is applied.

21. Use the **no ipx [*direction*]-sap-filter [#]** command, where *direction* is either input or output and # is the list number, to remove the list from the interface.

22. Type **exit** to return to global configuration mode.

23. Type **no access-list [#]**, where # is the list number, to remove the list from the router.

24. Exit to enable mode and use the **show access-lists** command to verify that the list has been removed.

25. Log out of the lab-e router.

Certification Objectives

Objectives for the CCNA exam:

➤ Monitor and verify selected access list operations on the router

Review Questions

1. What is the purpose of IPX SAP?

2. What is the default SAP update interval?

3. In the case of a SAP filter, what does the 0 in the access list represent?

4. Why are SAP filters important?

PPP AND ISDN

Labs included in this chapter

➤ Lab 11.1 Configure PPP with CHAP and PAP

➤ Lab 11.2 ISDN BRI Configuration

CCNA Exam Objectives	
Objective	**Lab**
Identify PPP operations to encapsulate WAN data on Cisco routers	11.1, 11.2
State a relevant use and context for ISDN networking	11.2
Identify ISDN protocols, function groups, reference points, and channels	11.2

LAB 11.1 CONFIGURE PPP WITH CHAP AND PAP

Objectives

The objective of this lab is to configure a serial interface on the router for Point-to-Point Protocol (PPP), with Challenge Handshake Authentication Protocol (CHAP) and Password Authentication Protocol (PAP) authentication. Although the default encapsulation on serial interfaces is High-level Data Link Control (HDLC), PPP is preferred in many cases because of its superior Network layer and authentication functionality.

In this lab you will configure each end of a WAN link for PPP with CHAP and PAP. *This means you must configure a router that has an active serial interface.* You will check the status of the newly configured serial interfaces using the show interface command. Finally, you will confirm Network layer connectivity between the WAN links.

After completing this lab you will be able to:

➤ Configure PPP with CHAP and PAP on a WAN link

➤ Understand why a WAN link is or is not operational

➤ Interpret the status line of the show interface command output

Materials Required

This lab requires the following:

➤ The internetworking lab setup used in the Chapter 6, 7, 8, and 9 labs

➤ Completion of the labs in Chapters 6 and 7

Estimated completion time: **30 minutes**

ACTIVITY

This lab cannot be done on the lab-e router because the router has no active serial interfaces.

1. Start the computer with Windows, and begin the HyperTerminal session with the router.

2. Turn on the routers and hubs, if necessary. Press **Enter** to get started, and then type the password **cisco** to reach the user EXEC mode prompt. Type **ena**, and then press **Enter** to access privileged EXEC mode.

3. Type **class**, and then press **Enter** when prompted for the enable secret password.

4. Enter global configuration mode.

5. Enter the command to configure an active serial interface on your router. Which command did you enter?

_____

6. Type **encap ppp**, and then press **Enter**. What does the "encap" abbreviation stand for?

_____

What does the encap ppp command do?

_____

What was the encapsulation before you changed it to ppp?

_____

7. Type **ppp auth chap pap**, and then press **Enter**. What does the "auth" abbreviation stand for?

_____

What does this command do?

_____

_____

8. Type **exit**, and then press **Enter** to return to global configuration mode.

9. Next, configure the username and password for the link. The command syntax is **username [*remote router hostname*] password [*password*]**. Use **cannon** as the password. Which command did you enter?

_____

10. Press **Ctrl+Z**.

11. Enter the **show interface** command for the interface that you just configured. What is the status of this interface?

_____

12. If the line protocol is down, what is your explanation for it being down? (*Hint:* is the other end of the WAN link configured for ppp?)

_____

_____

_____

13. Move to the remote router that you specified in Step 9. This router is on the other end of the WAN link that you just configured. To which router did you move?

_____

14. Enter global configuration mode, and then enter the command to configure the serial interface connected to the serial interface you have already configured. Which command did you enter?

_____

11

15. Type **encap ppp**, and then press **Enter**.

16. Type **ppp auth chap pap**, and then press **Enter**.

17. Press **Ctrl+Z**.

18. Enter the **show interface** command for the interface that you just configured. What is the status of this interface?

    _____

    _____

19. If the line protocol is down, what is your explanation for it being down? (*Hint*: password)

    _____

    _____

    _____

20. Enter global configuration mode.

21. Configure the username and password for the link, as you did in Step 9. You must use the remote router's hostname but the same password, which should be **cannon**. Which command did you enter?

    _____

22. Press **Ctrl+Z**.

23. Enter the **show interface** command again for the interface that you just configured. What is the status of this interface?

    _____

    _____

24. If the line protocol is up, what is your explanation?

    _____

    _____

    _____

25. Ping the other end of the WAN link to confirm connectivity. Which command did you use?

    _____

26. Enter the **show ip interface** command for the interface that you configured for PPP. Notice the words "peer address" with the IP address of the remote serial interface in the output. What is the meaning of the word "peer" in this context?

    _____

    _____

    _____

27. Enter global configuration mode, and then interface configuration mode for the serial interface on which the PPP encapsulation has been configured. Remove the PPP encapsulation from the serial interface. Which command did you use?

    _____

28. Exit to global configuration mode, and then use the keyboard and editing short-cuts to retrieve the username command and negate it.

29. Repeat Steps 27 and 28 for the first router that you configured for PPP. Exit to enable mode.

30. Use the **show interface** command to examine the default encapsulation on Cisco WAN interfaces. What is it?

_____

_____

31. Type **logout**, and then press **Enter** to exit the router.

Certification Objectives

Objectives for the CCNA exam:

➤ Identify PPP operations to encapsulate WAN data on Cisco routers

Review Questions

1. Why is PAP considered a two-way handshake?

2. Why is CHAP considered a three-way handshake?

3. When is Cisco's HDLC used on WAN interfaces?

4. What are the advantages of PPP compared to its predecessor SLIP?

LAB 11.2 ISDN BRI CONFIGURATION

Objectives

The objective of this lab is to configure global Integrated Services Digital Network (ISDN) parameters, identify and configure interesting traffic, configure Basic Rate Interface (BRI), and configure call information.

ISDN is a WAN service that is popular because of its relatively low cost as compared with the cost of a dedicated T1 line; therefore, it is an ideal backup or secondary link. The low cost is further reduced when ISDN BRI is configured using dial-on-demand routing (DDR).

11

In this lab you will configure the routers shown in Figure 11-1 for ISDN BRI with DDR. This includes CHAP authentication and static Internet Protocol (IP) route configuration.

After completing this lab you will be able to:

> ➤ Configure ISDN BRI

> ➤ Understand why configuring DDR reduces the cost of ISDN

> ➤ Understand that ISDN can use the PPP encapsulation method, which includes CHAP authentication

Materials Required

This lab requires the following:

> ➤ Pencil

Estimated completion time: **30 minutes**

ACTIVITY

1. Review Figure 11-1 before beginning this lab.

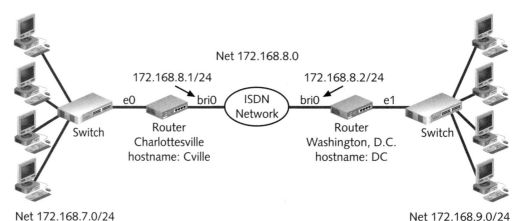

Figure 11-1   ISDN BRI example

2. The routers in Figure 11-1 have a bri0 interface. Are these routers TE1 devices or TE2 devices?

_____

Is a terminal adapter necessary between the routers and the telco BRI lines?

_____

Is an NT1 necessary between the routers and the telco BRI lines?

_____

What is the function of an NT1?

_____

3. In Figure 11-1, the computers off Charlottesville's e0 port require sporadic access to the server off Washington D.C.'s e1 port. This sporadic access does not justify the cost of a leased line. The alternative is to configure these routers to connect only when interesting traffic occurs. What is this configuration called?

_____

_____

4. The switch type in Figure 11-1 is an ni-1. Give the prompt and command to identify the switch type on the Charlottesville router, which has the hostname Cville.

_____

_____

5. What is the command to begin configuring the bri0 interface? To what does the prompt change?

_____

_____

6. What is the command to configure IP on the bri0 interface of the Cville router?

_____

7. What is the command to configure the spid number for spid number 1, which is 3535353535?

_____

8. What are the commands to configure PPP encapsulation with CHAP authentication on the Cville router?

_____

_____

9. What is the command to configure the dialer to map the Washington, D.C., bri0 interface to phone number (202) 555-1212 at a speed of 64 Kbps. The router's hostname is DC.

_____

10. What is the command to apply dialer-group 2 to Cville's bri0 interface?

_____

11. What is the command to force the line to disconnect if no interesting traffic occurs for 200 seconds?

_____

11

12. What is the dialer-list command that is paired with the dialer-group command? The dialer-list command should allow all IP traffic. Which prompt is used with the dialer-list command?

_____

_____

_____

13. What is the command to configure the username and password on the Cville router? The password is cvilledc.

_____

_____

14. What is the command to configure a static route on the Cville router to the DC LAN?

_____

Certification Objectives

Objectives for the CCNA exam:

➤ State a relevant use and context for ISDN networking

➤ Identify ISDN protocols, function groups, reference points, and channels

➤ Identify PPP operations to encapsulate WAN data on Cisco routers

Review Questions

1. How are the dialer-list/dialer-group commands similar to the access-list/access-group commands?

2. How does DDR save money?

3. Why is ISDN used most often with PPP encapsulation when HDLC encapsulation is the default serial encapsulation?

4. What is the advantage of using static rather than dynamic routing on the Cville router in this lab?

FRAME RELAY

Labs included in this chapter

➤ Lab 12.1 Set Up a Test Frame Relay Network

➤ Lab 12.2 Configure the Lab-c Router to Simulate a Frame Relay Switch

➤ Lab 12.3 Configure the Lab-b and Lab-d Routers for Frame Relay

CCNA Exam Objectives	
Objective	**Lab**
Recognize key Frame Relay terms and features	12.1, 12.2, 12.3
List commands to monitor Frame Relay operation in the router	12.3

LAB 12.1 SET UP A TEST FRAME RELAY NETWORK

Objectives

The objective of this lab is to configure a test Frame Relay network using a router to simulate the Frame Relay switch. As you may know, a Cisco router can be configured to act as a Frame Relay switch. Because a Frame Relay switch acts as a Channel Service Unit/Data Service Unit (CSU/DSU), the router simulating the switch must be configured as the data communications equipment (DCE) on both serial interfaces.

In this lab you will make the physical connections necessary to set up a test Frame Relay network. The lab-c router will act as the switch, and the lab-b and lab-d routers connected to the lab-c router will be configured for Frame Relay, as shown in Figure 12-1. You will also test the DCE.

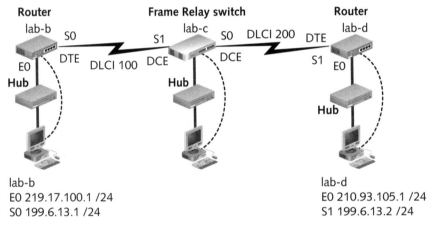

lab-b
EO 219.17.100.1 /24
SO 199.6.13.1 /24

lab-d
EO 210.93.105.1 /24
S1 199.6.13.2 /24

Figure 12-1   Frame Relay configuration

After completing this lab you will be able to:

> Set up a test Frame Relay network

> Understand the relationship between the DCE and the data terminal equipment (DTE) and the equipment that comprises each

> Test the DCE connection using the show controller serial command

> Erase the startup configuration on the routers

Materials Required

This lab requires the following:

> The internetworking lab setup used in the Chapter 6, 7, 8, and 9 labs

> Completion of the labs in Chapters 6 and 7

Estimated completion time: **30 minutes**

ACTIVITY

1. Make sure that all routers are off. Review Figure 12-1; it will be a reference tool while you are working through this lab.

2. Remove the serial cable between the lab-b and lab-c routers.

3. Plug the DCE end into the S1 interface of the lab-c router.

4. Plug the DTE end into the S0 interface of the lab-b router. Why is reversing the serial cable ends necessary in this lab?

   _____

   _____

5. Turn on the lab-b, lab-c, and lab-d routers and the hubs that are connected to them.

6. Turn on the computers connected via the console port to the three routers, if necessary.

7. Open a session in HyperTerminal to connect to the three routers.

8. Move to the lab-c router terminal, which will be the one simulating the Frame Relay switch.

9. Press **Enter** to get started, if necessary, and type the password **cisco** to reach the user EXEC mode prompt. Type **ena**, and then press **Enter** to access privileged EXEC mode.

10. Type **class**, and then press **Enter** when prompted for the enable secret password.

11. Type **show controller serial 0**, and then press **Enter**. Does the command output indicate that it is a DCE port?

    _____

    If the answer is no, something is wrong with the way the cable is connected to the S0 interface, and you must begin troubleshooting. Make sure the correct end of the cable is securely attached to the router interface. If the answer is yes, proceed to Step 12.

12. Type **show controller serial 1**, and then press **Enter**. Does the command output indicate that it is a DCE port?

    _____

    If the answer is no, something is wrong with the way that the cable is connected to the S1 interface, and you must begin troubleshooting. Make sure the correct end of the cable is securely attached to the router interface. If the answer is yes, proceed to Step 13.

12

13. Type **erase start**, and then press **Enter** to erase the startup configuration. Confirm the erase, if necessary. Where is the startup configuration stored?

_____

14. Type **reload**, and then press **Enter** to restart the router with the empty configuration. If you are prompted to save, press **N** for no. Confirm the reload.

15. Because the startup configuration has been erased, you will be prompted to enter an initial configuration using the System Configuration Dialog. Press **N** for no and press **Enter**. You may also be prompted to terminate autoinstall. Press **Y** for yes and press **Enter**.

16. Move to the lab-b router terminal.

17. Press **Enter** to get started if necessary, and then type the password **cisco** to reach the user EXEC mode prompt. Type **ena**, and then press **Enter** to access privileged EXEC mode.

18. Type **class**, and then press **Enter** when prompted for the enable secret password.

19. Type **show controller serial 0**, and then press **Enter**. Does the command output indicate that it is a DTE port?

_____

If the answer is no, something is wrong with the way the cable is connected to the S0 interface, and you must begin troubleshooting. If the answer is yes, proceed to Step 20.

20. Type **erase start**, and then press **Enter** to erase the startup configuration. Confirm the erase, if necessary.

21. Type **reload**, and then press **Enter** to restart the router with the empty configuration. If you are prompted to save, press **N** for no. Confirm the reload.

22. Because the startup configuration has been erased, you will be prompted to enter an initial configuration using the System Configuration Dialog. Press **N** for no and press **Enter**. You may also be prompted to terminate autoinstall. Press **Y** for yes and press **Enter**.

23. Move to the lab-d router terminal.

24. Press **Enter** to get started, if necessary, and type the password **cisco** to reach the user EXEC mode prompt. Type **ena**, and then press **Enter** to access privileged EXEC mode.

25. Type **class**, and then press **Enter** when prompted for the enable secret password.

26. Type **show controller serial 1**, and then press **Enter**. Does the command output indicate that it is a DTE port?

_____

If the answer is no, something is wrong with the way that the cable is connected to the S1 interface, and you must begin troubleshooting. If the answer is yes, proceed to Step 27.

27. Type **erase start**, and press **Enter** to erase the startup configuration. Confirm the erase, if necessary.

28. Type **reload**, and then press **Enter** to restart the router with the empty configuration. If you are prompted to save, press **N** for no. Confirm the reload.

29. Because the startup configuration has been erased, you will be prompted to enter an initial configuration using the System Configuration Dialog. Press **N** for no and press **Enter**. You may also be prompted to terminate autoinstall. Press **Y** for yes and press **Enter**.

30. In Frame Relay networks, what is the DCE?

    _____

    _____

    In Frame Relay networks, what is the DTE?

    _____

    _____

    You have now made and tested the physical connections necessary to make the lab-c router simulate a Frame Relay switch. In the next lab, you will configure the lab-c router with the correct Frame Relay commands.

Certification Objectives

Objectives for the CCNA exam:

➤ Recognize key Frame Relay terms and features

12

Review Questions

1. What is the function of a DTE?

2. What is the function of a DCE?

3. In the case of Frame Relay, are the DTE and DCE both customer premise equipment (CPE)?

LAB 12.2 CONFIGURE THE LAB-C ROUTER TO SIMULATE A FRAME RELAY SWITCH

Objectives

If you have made the physical connections as outlined in Lab 12.1, you are now ready to configure the lab-c router to simulate a Frame Relay switch, which is the objective of this lab. This lab involves some commands that, although not normally seen on a router, will give you insight into the structure of a Frame Relay network.

In this lab you will configure the lab-c router to simulate a Frame Relay switch that connects the lab-b and lab-d routers.

After completing this lab you will be able to:

➤ Configure a router to simulate a Frame Relay switch

➤ Understand how a Frame Relay switch operates

Materials Required

This lab requires the following:

➤ The internetworking lab setup used in the Chapter 6, 7, 8, and 9 labs

➤ Completion of the labs in Chapters 6 and 7, and Lab 12.1

Estimated completion time: **30 minutes**

ACTIVITY

1. Move to the lab-c router terminal, if necessary. Press **Enter** to get started, and then enter global configuration mode.

2. Type **fr switching**, and then press **Enter**. This command must be entered before the router can perform as a Frame Relay switch.

3. Type **int s1**, and then press **Enter** to begin configuration of the serial port leading to the lab-b router, as shown in Figure 12-1.

4. Type **encap fr**, and then press **Enter**. What does this command do?

_____

_____

5. Type **no ip address**, and then press **Enter**. Why is there no IP address on this router interface?

_____

_____

6. Type **clockrate 1000000**, and then press **Enter**. What is the speed of this link? (Include units in your speed statement.)

_____

Why is the clockrate command necessary on this interface?

_____

_____

7. Type **fr intf-type dce**, and then press **Enter**. This command sets up the interface as a DCE device on a Frame Relay network. The default is DTE, so you won't normally use this command on a router.

8. Type **fr route 100 int S0 200**, and then press **Enter**. This command configures a static route from the lab-b router to the lab-d router through the switch using the DLCIs.

9. Type **no shutdown** and then press **Enter**.

10. Enter interface configuration mode for the S0 interface, and configure it as you configured the S1 interface using the commands in Steps 4 through 9. The static route command in Step 8 will be slightly different, reflecting a route from the lab-d router to the lab-b router. Which static route command will you use?

_____

11. Press **Ctrl+Z** to exit to enable mode. In the next lab, you will configure the lab-b and lab-d routers to operate on the simulated Frame Relay network.

Certification Objectives

Objectives for the CCNA exam:

➤ Recognize key Frame Relay terms and features

Review Questions

1. Which WAN encapsulation was on the serial interface on the lab-c router before you configured it for Frame Relay?

2. Why don't you typically use the "fr switching" command on a router?

3. What does the Data Link Connection Identifier (DLCI) do?

4. What is the most important parameter to negotiate in a Frame Relay contract with a service provider?

LAB 12.3 CONFIGURE THE LAB-B AND LAB-D ROUTERS FOR FRAME RELAY

Objectives

If you have made the physical connections, as outlined in Lab 12.1, and configured the lab-c router to simulate a Frame Relay switch, as outlined in Lab 12.2, you are now ready to configure the lab-b and lab-d routers for Frame Relay, which is the objective of this lab.

In this lab you will configure the lab-b and lab-d routers for Frame Relay with the default cisco encapsulation for Local Management Interface (LMI) and Inverse ARP enabled. You will then test your configuration using the Frame Relay show commands.

After completing this lab you will be able to:

➤ Configure a router for Frame Relay

➤ Understand the output of the various Frame Relay show commands

Materials Required

This lab requires the following:

➤ The internetworking lab setup used in the Chapter 6, 7, 8, and 9 labs

➤ Completion of the labs in Chapters 6 and 7, and Labs 12.1 and 12.2

Estimated completion time: **30 minutes**

ACTIVITY

1. Move to the lab-b router terminal, if necessary, and then press **Enter** to get started and enter global configuration mode.

2. Configure the IP address on the E0 interface of the lab-b router, per Figure 12-1. Which command did you enter?

_____

3. Type **no shutdown** and press **Enter**.

4. Configure the IP address on the S0 interface of the lab-b router, per Figure 12-1. Include the no shutdown command. Which commands did you enter?

_____

5. Type **encap fr** and then press **Enter**. What does this command do?

_____

_____

6. Exit to global configuration mode.

7. Enter the command to configure the router for Interior Gateway Routing Protocol (IGRP) using the autonomous system number 20. Which command did you enter?

_____

8. Enter the **network** commands to complete the IGRP configuration. Use Figure 12-1 as a reference. Which two network commands did you enter?

_____

Notice that when the lab-c router operates as a Frame Relay switch, the serial interfaces on the lab-b and lab-d routers reside on the same network.

9. Press **Ctrl+Z** to return to enable mode.

10. Move to the lab-d router terminal.

11. Using Steps 2 through 9 and Figure 12-1 as a reference, configure the lab-d router for Frame Relay.

12. From the lab-d router, ping the Ethernet port of the lab-b router. Was the ping operation successful?

_____

If the answer is no, check your configurations on all three routers and get help from your teammates or instructor if necessary. Make sure that the interfaces are not shut down. In addition, check your routing table. There should be three entries in the routing table of the lab-d and lab-b routers: the two networks to which the router is directly connected and a network that the router learned about via IGRP. Repeat step 12 from the lab-b router and ping the lab-d router. When the ping operations are successful, proceed to Step 13.

13. Type **show fr pvc** on the lab-b or lab-d router, and then press **Enter**. Are these routers acting as DCEs or DTEs? How do you know?

_____

_____

What is the local DLCI?

_____

14. Type **show fr map** on the lab-b or lab-d router, and then press **Enter**. To which IP address is the local DLCI mapped?

_____

15. Type **show interface** on the lab-b or lab-d router. Can you verify that the Frame Relay encapsulation is on the appropriate serial interface?

_____

12

16. Move to the lab-c router console terminal.

17. Type **show fr route**, and then press **Enter** to look at the Frame Relay switching table. What information is contained in a Frame Relay switch table?

_____

_____

_____

18. Type **show fr pvc**, and then press **Enter** on the lab-c router terminal. Is this router acting as a DCE or DTE? How do you know?

_____

_____

19. Log out of all three routers. Turn off the three routers.

20. Switch the ends of the serial cable between the lab-b and lab-c router.

Certification Objectives

Objectives for the CCNA exam:

➤ Recognize key Frame Relay terms and features

➤ List commands to monitor Frame Relay operation in the router

Review Questions

1. Which show command displays statistics regarding the pvc circuit?

2. How exactly did the Frame Relay map table get built in this lab?

3. Why didn't you have to use the "frame-relay lmi-type" command in this lab?

SWITCHING AND VLANs

Labs included in this chapter

➤ Lab 13.1 Configure a Cisco 1900 Switch Using the Menus

➤ Lab 13.2 Configure a Cisco 1900 Switch Using the Command-Line Interface

➤ Lab 13.3 Evaluate Hub Performance

➤ Lab 13.4 Evaluate Switch Performance

➤ Lab 13.5 Understanding Switching and LAN Design Concepts and Terminology

---

CCNA Exam Objectives	
Objective	**Lab**
Name and describe two switching methods	13.1, 13.2, 13.5
Distinguish between cut-through and store-and-forward LAN switching	13.1, 13.2, 13.5
Describe the operation of the Spanning Tree Protocol and its benefits	13.1, 13.2
Describe the benefits of virtual LANs	13.1, 13.2
Describe full- and half-duplex Ethernet operation	13.3, 13.4, 13.5
Describe network congestion problems in Ethernet networks	13.3, 13.4, 13.5
Describe the features and benefits of Fast Ethernet	13.5
Describe the guidelines and distance limitations of Fast Ethernet	13.5
Describe LAN segmentation using switches	13.4, 13.5
Describe the benefits of network segmentation with switches	13.4, 13.5

LAB 13.1 CONFIGURE A CISCO 1900 SWITCH USING THE MENUS

Objectives

The Cisco 1900 switch can be configured in various ways. You can use the menu or the command line interface (CLI) when connected via a console cable, or you can use the visual switch manager via a web browser.

The objective of this lab is for you to become familiar with the 1900 switch series by connecting a terminal to the switch and configuring basic settings using the menus. The Catalyst 1900 series switches have twelve or twenty-four 10-Mbps ports for 10BaseT devices and one 10-Mbps AUI port. In addition to these interfaces, the 1900 provides two 100BaseT ports. The switch has a console port like a router so that it can be configured via a PC by using programs such as HyperTerminal.

In this lab you will connect a workstation to a 1900 series switch via the console port. Next, you will configure HyperTerminal to access the switch. Finally, you will configure the switch using the Management Console, which is a menu-driven configuration utility.

After completing this lab you will be able to:

➤ Physically connect a Cisco 1900 series switch to a workstation for configuration purposes

➤ Configure the HyperTerminal program to access the switch configuration

➤ Configure the VLANs and set the switching mode using the switch's Management Console utility

➤ Configure a console password on the switch

➤ Reset the switch configuration to factory defaults

Materials Required

This lab requires the following:

➤ One Cisco 1900 series switch with Enterprise Edition software

➤ Power cord for switch

➤ One Windows PC with the HyperTerminal program installed

➤ Console cable for the switch

➤ RJ-45-to-DB-9 or-DB-25 adapter

Estimated completion time: **45 minutes**

ACTIVITY

1. Make sure that the workstation is off.

2. Make sure that the Cisco switch is off. There is no power button on the switch; you have to unplug it to turn it off.

3. Connect one end of the console cable to the console port on the switch.

4. Connect the other end of the cable to the COM1 or COM2 port on the Windows PC. You will need an RJ-45-to-DB-9 or-DB-25 adapter on the PC end of the cable.

5. Plug in the switch and turn on the computer. Wait for the port lights located on the front of the switch, to go out before continuing.

6. Click **Start**, click **Programs**, click **Accessories**, click **Communications**, and then click the **HyperTerminal** program. Double-click the **Hypertrm** program. Click the **File** menu, and then click **New Connection** if this window does not come up by itself.

7. Type **SWITCH** in the Name text box, and then press **Enter**.

8. If you are prompted to install a modem, click **No**.

9. In the Connect using: box, choose **Direct to COM1** or **Direct to COM2**, depending on whether your cable is connected to the COM1 or COM2 port. Click **OK**.

10. Enter the settings as you would when connecting to a Cisco router. In other words, enter the following settings in the appropriate text boxes:
    Bits per Second = **9600**; Data Bits = **8**; Parity = **None**;
    Stop Bits = **1**; Flow Control = **Hardware**

11. Click **OK** to accept the configuration.

12. If there is no response from the switch in the HyperTerminal window, press **Enter**. If it still does not work, ask your instructor or a classmate for help with the configuration. You may have made incorrect cable connections. If you receive a response from the switch, proceed to Step 13.

13. The User Interface menu should be displayed. Type **M** to access the switch via the menu interface.

14. The main menu of the switch's Management Console should now be displayed. Type **C** to set a console password.

15. At this time, there is probably no password set. It is important to be very careful when setting a switch password. There is no password recovery routine as there is on a Cisco router. Type **M** to modify the password.

16. Type **cisco** for the password, and then press **Enter**. Type **cisco** again to verify the password, and then press **Enter**.

17. Press any key to continue, and then type **X** to exit to the main menu.

18. Type **S** to access the system configuration menu.

19. Type **N** to name the switch, and then type **Cisco1900** and press **Enter**.

20. Type **C**, and then enter *your name* as the contact name.

21. Type **L**, and then enter **PVCC room 180** as the location.

22. Type **S**, and then set the switching mode to **store-and-forward** by typing a **1** and pressing **Enter**. What is the default switching mode on the Cisco 1900 series switch?

_____

23. Type **X** to exit to the main menu.

24. Type **N** to access the network management menu.

25. Type **B** to investigate the Spanning Tree Protocol settings. Is STP enabled by default?

_____

13

26. Type **X** to exit to the previous menu level, and then type **X** again to exit to the main menu.
27. Type **V** to access the VLAN menu.
28. Press **A** to add a VLAN.
29. Type **1**, and then press **Enter** to choose the Ethernet VLAN type.
30. Type **V** for VLAN name, type **Engineering** when prompted for the VLAN name, and then press **Enter** to name the second VLAN Engineering.
31. Type **S** to save and exit.

How many local VLANs are supported by the switch?

_____

32. Type **A** to add another VLAN.
33. Type **1**, and then press **Enter** to configure the VLAN for Ethernet.
34. Type **N**, type **3**, and press **Enter** to create VLAN 3.
35. Type **V** to name the VLAN, and then type **Finance** and press **Enter**.
36. Type **S** to save and exit.
37. Type **L** to list your VLANs. Type **1, 2, 3** and press **Enter** to list VLANs 1, 2, and 3. What is the name of VLAN 1?

_____

What is the name of VLAN 2?

_____

What is the name of VLAN 3?

_____

If the VLANs do not display correctly, attempt to reconfigure them using Steps 27 through 36.
38. Press any key to continue if instructed to do so.
39. Type **E** for VLAN membership. Have any ports been assigned to the Engineering or Finance VLANs?

_____

40. Type **V** for VLAN assignment.
41. Type **4–8**, press **Enter**, and then type **2** to move ports 4–8 to the Engineering VLAN. Press **Enter** again.
42. Repeat Steps 40 and 41, but this time move ports **9–12** to VLAN 3.
43. Type **X** to exit to the previous menu.
44. Type **X** to exit to the main menu, and then type **X** again to log out of the management console.
45. Type **Y** and press **Enter** to confirm.
46. Type **M** to attempt to return to the switch menu interface. Were you prompted for a password?

_____

If you were prompted for a password, type **cisco** and press **Enter**.

47. Type **S** for system, and then type **F** to reset the factory defaults of the switch. Type **Y**, and then press **Enter** to confirm.
48. Close HyperTerminal. Save the switch settings when prompted.
49. Unplug the switch.
50. Remove the console cable from the switch and the PC.

Certification Objectives

Objectives for the CCNA exam:
- ➤ Name and describe two switching methods
- ➤ Distinguish between cut-through and store-and-forward LAN switching
- ➤ Describe the operation of the Spanning Tree Protocol and its benefits
- ➤ Describe the benefits of virtual LANs

Review Questions

1. What is the difference between cut-through and store-and-forward switching?

2. Why is fragment-free somewhere between cut-through and store-and-forward in terms of speed and error detection?

3. What do you need to facilitate traffic between different VLANs?

4. What is the benefit of grouping switch ports into different VLANs?

13

LAB 13.2 CONFIGURE A CISCO 1900 SWITCH USING THE COMMAND LINE INTERFACE

Objectives

The objective of this lab is to configure a Cisco 1900 series switch using the command-line interface. Using commands rather than the menus provides exposure to an additional way to configure a Cisco switch. Switch commands are part of the CCNA exam.

After completing this lab you will be able to:
- ➤ Identify the status of switch ports
- ➤ Configure the hostname, IP address, gateway, and domain name on the switch
- ➤ Examine the Spanning Tree Protocol settings
- ➤ Configure port security
- ➤ Change the switching type
- ➤ Configure a new VLAN
- ➤ Configure VTP

➤ Modify the CDP parameters
➤ Copy the switch configuration to a TFTP server
➤ Reset the switch configuration to factory defaults

Materials Required

This lab requires the following:

➤ One Cisco 1900 series switch with Enterprise Edition IOS
➤ A console cable for the switch
➤ RJ-45-to-DB-9 or-DB-25 adapter
➤ Three Windows workstations with NIC cards installed and with HyperTerminal installed (it is easiest to use the lab-d, lab-e, and TFTP server computers)
➤ One of the computers must be running TFTP software and be configured with IP address 210.93.105.3.
➤ The computer known as lab-d should be configured for IP address 210.93.105.4
➤ The computer known as lab-e should be configured for IP address 210.93.105.5
➤ Two patch cables
➤ One power cord for the switch

> Estimated completion time: **60 minutes**

ACTIVITY

1. Review Figure 13-1. Plug the console cable into the Cisco 1900 switch console port.

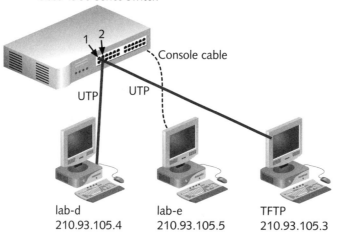

Figure 13-1   Lab 13.2 configuration

2. Plug the other end of the console cable into an RJ45-to-DB9 or RJ45-to-DB25 adapter and connect the adapter to a COM port on the lab-e computer.

3. Connect the TFTP server with IP address 210.93.105.3 to **port 1** of the switch with a UTP patch cable.

4. Connect the lab-d computer with IP address 210.93.105.4 to **port 2** of the switch with a UTP patch cable.

5. Turn on the TFTP server if necessary.

6. Turn on the lab-d computer if necessary.

7. Plug in the switch.

8. The port lights on the switch should turn green and all lights should initially be on and not blinking. After a minute or so, port lights without connections should go off. Ports 1 and 2 should turn first to orange and then to green, which indicates readiness. If the port lights with the computer connections are orange and do not turn green, there is a problem, possibly with the cable. Start troubleshooting and ask your instructor for help.

9. On the lab-d computer, click **Start**, point to **Programs**, and then click **MS-DOS prompt**.

10. Type **ping 210.93.105.3** and press **Enter**.

11. Were you able to ping the TFTP server successfully?

_____

If you were not able to ping successfully, start troubleshooting with the help of your instructor.

12. On the TFTP server, click **Start**, point to **Programs**, and then click **MS-DOS prompt**.

13. Type **ping 210.93.105.4** and press **Enter**.

14. Were you able to ping the lab-d computer successfully?

_____

If you were not able to ping successfully, start troubleshooting with the help of your instructor.

15. Turn on the lab-e computer if necessary.

16. Click **Start**, point to **Programs**, point to **Accessories**, point to **Communications**, and then click **Hyperterminal**. Double-click a saved HyperTerminal connection if there is one. If there is no saved Hyperterminal connection on your computer, create one using the instructions in Lab 13.1, Steps 6 through 11.

17. Press **Enter** to generate output from the switch, if necessary.

18. Enter **K** to access the command-line interface. What is the prompt?

_____

What is the mode?

_____

19. Enter the **enable** command. What is the prompt?

_____

20. Enter global configuration mode using the **configure terminal** command. What is the prompt?

_____

13

21. Type **hostname malabar** and press **Enter**. What is the prompt?

    _____

22. Type **ip address 210.93.105.10 255.255.255.0** and press **Enter**.
23. Type **ip default-gateway 210.93.105.1** and press **Enter**.
24. Type **ip domain-name cannonball.com** and press **Enter**.
25. Press **Ctrl+Z** to return to enable mode.
26. Enter the **show ip** command. Does your IP configuration reflect the commands you entered in this section?

    _____

    If the answer is no, try entering your configuration again.
27. Enter the **show mac-address-table** command. How did the switching table get these MAC addresses?

    _____

    _____

28. Enter global configuration mode using the **configure terminal** command.
29. Enter the **interface e0/1** command to access the Ethernet port. Notice the slot type of "0" is included to reference the interface on this device. All commands entered at this point will affect which port number on the switch?

    _____

30. Type **port secure max-mac-count 1** and press **Enter**. What is the purpose of this command?

    _____

31. Enter **exit** to move back to global configuration mode.
32. Enter the **interface e0/2** command.
33. Use the **up arrow** to retrieve the **port secure max-mac-count 1** command and press **Enter**.
34. Press **Ctrl+Z** to return to enable mode.
35. Examine the Spanning Tree Protocol settings using the **show spantree 1** command. What does the "1" in the command designate?

    _____

    _____

36. According to the show spantree 1 command, what are ports 1 through 12 doing?

    _____

    _____

    _____

37. What are ports 25, 26, and 27 doing?

    _____

    _____

    _____

38. What kind of port is port 25 on the Cisco 1900?

    _____

39. What kind of port is port 26 on the Cisco 1900?

_____

40. What kind of port is port 27 on the Cisco 1900?

_____

41. Enter the **show interface** command. What is the status of ports 1 and 2?

_____

What is the status of ports 3 through 12?

_____

What is the status of port 25?

_____

What is the status of port 26 and 27?

_____

42. Enter the **show port system** command. What is the default switching mode of the Cisco 1900 switch?

_____

43. Enter global configuration mode.
44. Type **switching-mode store-and-forward** and press **Enter**.
45. Press **Ctrl+Z**.
46. Type **show port system** and press **Enter**. Did the switching mode change as directed?

_____

47. Enter the **configure terminal** command to enter global configuration mode.
48. Type **vtp server** and press **Enter**.
49. Type **vtp domain cannonball** and press **Enter**. Why do you need to create a VTP domain?

_____

_____

50. Press **Ctrl+Z** to return to enable mode.
51. Enter the **show vtp** command. Is the switch operating as a VTP server?

_____

52. Enter the **configure terminal** command again to enter global configuration mode.
53. Enter the **interface f 0/26** command. What does the "f" represent?

_____

What does the "0" represent?

_____

What does the "26" represent?

_____

54. Type **trunk on** and press **Enter**. What does this command do?

_____

_____

13

55. Press **Ctrl+Z** to return to enable mode.
56. Type the **show vlan 1** command and press **Enter**. Are all ports on VLAN 1?

_____

57. Enter the **configure terminal** command again to enter global configuration mode.
58. Type the **vlan 2 name cannon** command, and press **Enter**. What does this do?

_____

59. Enter the **interface e0/2** command.
60. Enter the **vlan-membership static 2** command.
61. Press **Ctrl+Z** to return to enable mode.
62. Type **show vlan** and press **Enter**. VLAN 2 should be named "cannon" and port 2 should now be assigned to VLAN2. Does the output look correct?

_____

If not, attempt to reconfigure the VLAN by returning to Step 57 and redoing the VLAN configuration.

63. Type **show vlan-membership** and press **Enter**. What is the difference between this command and the show vlan command?

_____

_____

64. Type **ping 210.93.105.3** and press **Enter**. Were you able to successfully ping the TFTP server from the switch?

_____

65. Move to the lab-d computer, click **Start**, point to **Programs**, and then click **MS-DOS Prompt**. Type **ping 210.93.105.3** and press **Enter**. Were you able to successfully ping the TFTP server from the lab-d computer?

_____

Why or why not?

_____

_____

66. Move the patch cable for the lab-d computer from port 2 on the switch to port 3. Now, attempt to ping the TFTP server from the lab-d computer again. The IP address is 210.93.105.3. Was the ping successful? Why or why not?

_____

_____

67. Return to the lab-e computer and the switch. Enter the **show cdp** command. What is the broadcast interval?

_____

What is the holdtime?

_____

68. Enter global configuration mode.
69. Enter the **cdp timer 90** command.
70. Enter the **cdp holdtime 240** command.
71. Press **Ctrl+Z**.
72. Enter the **show cdp** command. Did the timer information change per your commands?

    _____

    If not, redo the commands in this section, beginning with Step 68.
73. Make sure you can ping the TFTP server at 210.93.105.3 from the switch.
74. Open the TFTP server software on the TFTP server if necessary.
75. Backup the switch configuration to the TFTP using the following command at the enable mode prompt:

    copy nvram tftp://210.93.105.3/1900switch
76. If the copy was successful, you will receive a message indicating success. Was it successful?

    _____

    What does the "1900switch" in the command designate?

    _____

    Could you have used a different name?

    _____

77. Reset the configuration to the factory defaults using the **delete nvram** command in enable mode. Press **Y** for yes and press **Enter** to confirm the deletion.
78. Unplug the switch and remove the patch cables from the switch ports.

Certification Objectives

Objectives for the CCNA exam:
➤ Name and describe two switching methods
➤ Distinguish between cut-through and store-and-forward LAN switching
➤ Describe the operation of the Spanning Tree Protocol and its benefits
➤ Describe the benefits of virtual LANs

Review Questions

1. What is the function of a VTP server?

2. What is the VLAN limit on the Cisco 1900 series switch?

3. How many VLANs can STP support on one 1900 series switch?

13

4. What is a port doing if it is in the forwarding state?

5. What is a port doing if it is in the blocking state?

6. Can you delete a VLAN 1? Why or why not?

7. Is CDP enabled by default on the Cisco 1900 series switch?

LAB 13.3 EVALUATE HUB PERFORMANCE

Objectives

The objective of this lab is to illustrate how hubs operate given two different scenarios. The first scenario involves generating data traffic on two ports. The second scenario involves generating data traffic on all active ports.

In this lab you will connect the six computers used in the internetworking lab to a common hub. Next, you will time the transfer of a large folder of files between two of the computers. Finally, you will measure the time it takes to move the folder back to its original location while generating traffic on the rest of the network.

The workstations used in this lab are the same ones used to connect to the lab-a through lab-e routers, inclusive. As such, the workstations are referred to as the lab-a workstation, the lab-b workstation, and so on. The TFTP server workstation is also used.

After completing this lab you will be able to:

➤ Describe how hubs perform when transferring data between two computers
➤ Describe how hubs perform when transferring data between many computers

Materials Required

This lab requires the following:

➤ The internetworking lab computers: lab-a, lab-b, lab-c, lab-d, lab-e, and the TFTP server
➤ Lab workstations with IP addresses configured for the 210.93.105.0 network and with all workstations in the same workgroup
➤ One hub
➤ Six UTP patch cables
➤ A shared desktop on all computers with full access
➤ A folder named SWITCHTEST containing enough files to equal at least 100 MB on the desktops of the lab-b, lab-d, and lab-e computers
➤ A stopwatch

Estimated completion time: **30 minutes**

ACTIVITY

1. Turn on the lab workstations, if necessary.
2. Review Figure 13-2. Connect all six workstations via UTP from their NICs to a single hub. Make sure that you do not use the uplink port on the hub. Make sure that the hub lights are on.

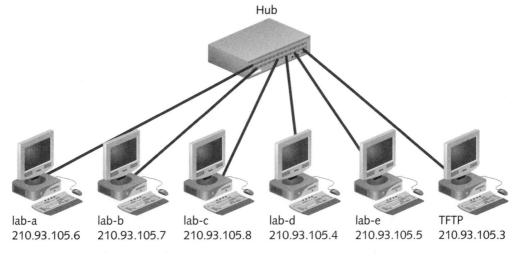

Hub

lab-a	lab-b	lab-c	lab-d	lab-e	TFTP
210.93.105.6	210.93.105.7	210.93.105.8	210.93.105.4	210.93.105.5	210.93.105.3

Figure 13-2   Lab 13.3 configuration

13

3. Double-click **Network Neighborhood** on all computers to make sure that every workstation can see every other workstation in the lab setup, including the TFTP server. Sometimes it takes awhile for the computers to see each other. If every workstation is not visible in Network Neighborhood, contact your instructor.
4. Move to the TFTP server, double-click **Network Neighborhood**, double-click the **lab-e** icon, and then double-click the **Desktop** folder.
5. Right-drag the **SWITCHTEST** folder from the desktop of the lab-e computer to the desktop of the TFTP server. *When the quick menu pops up, stop. This is the operation that you will time using the stopwatch.*
6. Using the stopwatch, calculate the time that it takes to move the SWITCHTEST folder from the lab-e computer to the TFTP server.
7. You and your team should watch the move operation and be prepared to type **A** for All if you are prompted for a confirmation regarding the move.
8. Observe the hub during the move. If there is a collision light, how active is it?

_____

_____

9. Observe the NICs on the six computers. Is there any appreciable activity on the NICs of workstations that are not participating in the move?

_____

10. How long (in minutes and seconds) did it take to move the SWITCHTEST folder from the lab-e computer to the TFTP server?

_____

11. Prepare to move the SWITCHTEST folder simultaneously from the TFTP server to the lab-e computer, from the lab-d computer to the lab-c computer, and from the lab-b computer to the lab-a computer.

12. Move to the lab-c computer, double-click **Network Neighborhood**, double-click the **lab-d** icon, and then double-click the **Desktop** folder. You should see the SWITCHTEST folder.

13. Right-drag the **SWITCHTEST** folder from the desktop of the lab-d computer to the desktop of your computer, which is lab-c. When the quick menu pops up, *stop*.

14. Move to the lab-a computer and repeat what you did in Steps 12 and 13 in preparation for moving the SWITCHTEST folder from the lab-b desktop to the desktop of the lab-a computer.

15. Move to the lab-e computer and repeat Steps 12 and 13 in preparation for moving the SWITCHTEST folder from the TFTP server to the desktop of the lab-e computer. *This is the only operation that you will time using the stopwatch.*

16. As close to simultaneously as possible, have your team begin moving the SWITCHTEST folder from the lab-d computer to the lab-c computer, from the lab-b computer to the lab-a computer, and from the TFTP server to the lab-e computer. *Remember that one of the team members must time the move from the TFTP server to the lab-e computer.*

17. You and your team should watch the move operations and be prepared to type **A** for All if you are prompted for a confirmation regarding the move. You want to keep traffic moving.

18. Observe the hub during the move. If there is a collision light, how active is it compared with when you generated activity on only two ports?

_____

_____

19. Approximately how long did it take (in minutes and seconds) to move the SWITCHTEST folder from the TFTP server to the lab-e computer?

_____

20. Compare your answer in Step 19 with your answer in Step 10. If there is a difference, how do you account for it?

_____

_____

_____

Certification Objectives

Objectives for the CCNA exam:

➤ Describe full- and half-duplex Ethernet operation

➤ Describe network congestion problems in Ethernet networks

Review Questions

1. How does regular half-duplex communications through a hub work?

2. Would a hub be used to solve network congestion problems in an Ethernet network? Why or why not?

3. Why did it take so much longer to transfer the files when there was traffic on all connected hub ports?

LAB 13.4 EVALUATE SWITCH PERFORMANCE

Objectives

The objective of this lab is to illustrate how switches operate in the two scenarios in which you worked in Lab 13.3. In this lab you will connect the six computers in the internetworking lab to a Cisco 1900 series switch and time the transfer of a large folder between two of the computers. You will then measure the time it takes to move the folder back while generating other traffic on the rest of the network. Finally, a comparison will be made between the times recorded in this lab and the times recorded for the hub in Lab 13.3.

After completing this lab you will be able to:

➤ Understand how switches perform when transferring data between two computers
➤ Understand how switches perform when transferring data between many computers

13

Materials Required

This lab requires the following:

➤ The internetworking lab computers: lab-a, lab-b, lab-c, lab-d, lab-e, and the TFTP server
➤ Lab workstations with IP addresses configured for the 210.93.105.0 network
➤ One Cisco 1900 series switch
➤ Six UTP patch cables
➤ A shared desktop on all computers with full access
➤ A folder named SWITCHTEST containing enough files to equal at least 100 MB on the desktops of the lab-b, lab-d, and lab-e computers
➤ A stopwatch
➤ The completion of Lab 13.3

Estimated completion time: **30 minutes**

ACTIVITY

1. Turn on the lab workstations, if necessary.
2. Review Figure 13-3. Connect all six workstations via UTP from their NICs to a single switch. Use **ports 5** and **6** for the lab-e computer and the TFTP server. Make sure that the switch is turned on and that the port lights on the switch have turned green.

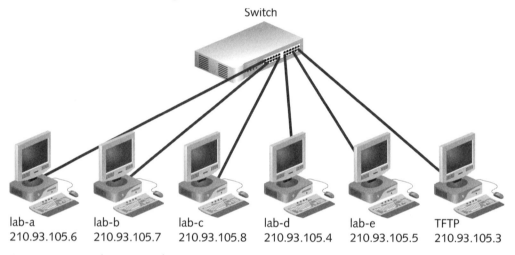

Switch

lab-a	lab-b	lab-c	lab-d	lab-e	TFTP
210.93.105.6	210.93.105.7	210.93.105.8	210.93.105.4	210.93.105.5	210.93.105.3

Figure 13-3   Lab 13.4 configuration

3. Double-click **Network Neighborhood** on all computers to make sure that every workstation can see every other workstation in the lab setup, including the TFTP server. Sometimes it takes awhile for all computers to see each other. If every workstation is not visible in Network Neighborhood, contact your instructor.
4. Move to the TFTP server, double-click **Network Neighborhood**, double-click the **lab-e** icon, and then double-click the **Desktop** folder.
5. Right-drag the **SWITCHTEST** folder from the desktop of the lab-e computer to the desktop of the TFTP server. When the quick menu pops up, *stop. This is the operation that you will time using the stopwatch.*
6. Using the stopwatch, calculate the time it takes to move the SWITCHTEST folder from the lab-e computer to the TFTP server.
7. You and your team should watch the move operation and be prepared to type **A** for All if you are prompted for a confirmation regarding the move.
8. Observe the switch during the move. Is there equal activity on each port, or are ports 5 and 6 busier than the other occupied ports?

9. Observe the NICs on the six computers. Is there any appreciable activity on the NICs of workstations not participating in the move?

_____

10. How long (in minutes and seconds) did it take to move the SWITCHTEST folder from the lab-e computer to the TFTP server?

_____

11. Prepare to move the SWITCHTEST folder simultaneously from the TFTP server to the lab-e computer, from the lab-c computer to the lab-d computer, and from the lab-a computer to the lab-b computer.

12. Move to the lab-d computer, double-click **Network Neighborhood**, double-click the **lab-c** icon, and then double-click the **desktop** folder. You should see the SWITCHTEST folder.

13. Right-drag the **SWITCHTEST** folder from the desktop of the lab-c computer to the desktop of your computer (lab-d). When the quick menu pops up, *stop*.

14. Move to the lab-b computer and repeat what you did in Steps 12 and 13 in preparation for moving the SWITCHTEST folder from the lab-a desktop to the desktop of the lab-b computer.

15. Move to the lab-e computer and repeat Steps 12 and 13 in preparation for moving the SWITCHTEST folder from the TFTP server to the desktop of the lab-e computer. *This is the only operation that you will time using the stopwatch.*

16. As close to simultaneously as possible, have your team begin moving the SWITCHTEST folder from the lab-c computer to the lab-d computer, from the lab-a computer to the lab-b computer, and from the TFTP server to the lab-e computer. *Remember that one of the team members must time the move from the TFTP server to the lab-e computer.*

17. You and your team should watch the move operations and be prepared to type **A** for All if you are prompted for a confirmation regarding the move. You want to keep traffic moving.

18. Observe the switch during the move. Is there equal activity on each connected port?

_____

19. Approximately how long did it take (in minutes and seconds) to move the SWITCHTEST folder from the TFTP server to the lab-e computer?

_____

20. Record your timings from Lab 13.3 and Lab 13.4 in Table 13-1:

Table 13-1   Hub and Switch Comparison

Scenario	Transfer Time in Minutes and Seconds
Hub—activity on two ports	
Hub—activity on six ports	
Switch—activity on two ports	
Switch—activity on six ports	

13

21. There should be a time difference between the two hub experiments. How do you explain this?

_____

_____

_____

22. There should be no appreciable time difference between the switch experiments. How do you explain this?

_____

_____

_____

23. If there was very little time difference between the hub and switch for the two-port activity experiments, how do you explain this?

_____

Certification Objectives

Objectives for the CCNA exam:
- ➤ Describe full- and half-duplex Ethernet operation
- ➤ Describe network congestion problems in Ethernet networks
- ➤ Describe LAN segmentation using switches
- ➤ Describe the benefits of network segmentation with switches

Review Questions

1. In terms of collisions and speed, what are the differences between hubs and switches?

2. How do switches solve network congestion problems on Ethernet networks?

3. What does the term "switched bandwidth" mean?

LAB 13.5 UNDERSTANDING SWITCHING AND LAN DESIGN CONCEPTS AND TERMINOLOGY

Objectives

The objective of this lab is to make sure you have a good understanding of modern Ethernet LAN design and the associated terminology. In this lab you will match switching and LAN design terms, which are in a bulleted list, with definitions in Table 13-2. After completing this lab you will:
- ➤ Understand the terms and concepts related to switching and LAN design.